Praise for *Unreachable*

"Mohan challenges us to rise above AI fear and obsession to become AI-enabled innovators who shape the future on our terms."

—Tony Robbins, #1 *New York Times* best-selling author, peak performance strategist, entrepreneur, philanthropist

"In an era dominated by AI, Mohan Nair reminds us of the irreplaceable power of human insight and creativity. This book is a masterful guide to reclaiming our innovative selves while embracing the transformative potential of AI."

—Lee Shapiro, managing partner, 7wire Ventures

"Thoughtfully provocative, *Unreachable* offers a counterbalance to the AI hysteria flooding the business world. It's not about rejecting the future as much as it's about surviving it intact."

—Caryn Lusinchi, AI governance and risk management expert, Global Governance Institute

"In *Unreachable*, there is a powerful correlate between man and machine that Mohan illuminates that the media is not adequately addressing. We are all fascinated by the capabilities of Gen AI, arguably dazzled by them, but have not focused the profoundly misunderstood potential implications."

—Michael A. Greeley, general partner, Flare Capital Partners

"Mohan's *Unreachable* challenges each of us to rethink our role as consumers of AI. We have a choice: either remain passive and fall behind in a world that is becoming ever more reliant on AI or take an active role in understanding how AI may complement our work and our lives. *Unreachable* makes a compelling case for the latter and provides valuable guidance for how to thrive in the era of AI."

—**David C. Rhew,** MD, global chief medical officer
and VP of healthcare, Microsoft

"*Unreachable* by Mohan Nair, a modern-day DaVinci (he is an artist and scientist), is about #AI and #insight and is a must-read for anyone wondering about the future of #innovation in the age of AI!"

—**Naomi Fried,** PhD, founder and CEO, PharmStars;
general partner, PharmStars Ventures

Unreachable

Unreachable

How Not to Lose Your Mind

in an **AI-Obsessed Era**

Mohan Nair

FC

**FAST
COMPANY**
Press

Fast Company Press
New York, New York
www.fastcompanypress.com

Distributed by River Grove Books

Design and composition by Greenleaf Book Group
Cover design by Greenleaf Book Group

Publisher's Cataloging-in-Publication data is available.

Print ISBN: 978-1-63908-168-4

Hardcover ISBN: 978-1-63908-170-7

eBook ISBN: 978-1-63908-169-1

First Edition

To my mother, who taught me grace,
imagination, curiosity, and endless love.

Contents

Preface

Unreachable is about the incredible opportunity given to us in the era of generative AI (Gen AI), the reality of Gen AI's unexpected cognitive side effects, and the discovery of an antidote to AI-obsession. Using the innovative capabilities within us, we can generate insights beyond the AI machine. Gen AI has both tremendous benefits and risks. This book celebrates Gen AI but provides a nutrition label to decreasing your attention, thinking, and memory. Let's call this your computational brain. You may lose your computational brain to AI, but this book will help you keep your insight-centered mind intact. *Unreachable* is about liberating your ability to generate your own aha moments on demand, anytime you wish to bring an idea to market. This, I theorize, will define the human contributive value of the future.

Human beings are innovators who can create transformational solutions. Humans have been around for 200,000 years, and we can tap into that vast history of experience to design the future and make it real. We can create a nonobvious future—one that is not an incremental change from our present but is a great leap forward and holds ideas that have never been experienced before. We humans are explorers of an unknown future. Our genetics give us the ability to tap into our future-focused innovative mind.

Do you wonder whether we will be significantly affected by AI? Not just by AI taking or eliminating our jobs, but by AI outsmarting us, eroding our brains, and leaving us behind? I have spent years exploring this impact. I believe humans have to rise above AI or be forgotten victims of the next era. The victims of the next era will be either overindulgent with AI, AI-obsessed, or fearful and avoiding (AI-afraid). This book describes the paths I have researched, experimented with, and followed as I sought to explore how we humans can evolve and dominate in a world with Gen AI.

Before we continue, do not think me anti-AI. I am a fan, and I believe AI has profound value. My professional experiences have given me a unique vantage point on this issue. I have spent decades leading transformational innovation endeavors for large companies and governments and experiencing the successful results of those projects. I have spent decades in technology development at a level that few have the opportunity to experience. And, above all, I have been a human being for most, if not all, of my life!

Think of this book as a nutrition label that will allow you to protect your focused attention, thinking abilities, learning and growth in an AI-obsessed era. Nutrition labels are not meant to stop you. They are meant to warn you and protect your health from overindulgence. If we fail at this, we fall prey to unexpected disadvantages. In addition to warning you, I hope to inspire you to take advantage of the amazing opportunity Gen AI affords us to become our best innovative selves.

One current advantage human beings have over Gen AI is that humans are semantic beings who find meaning, unlike AI, which is a term that comprises syntactic non-beings that understand life by digesting texts, sounds, and videos. Humans, unlike machines, develop thoughts and actions based on the meaning of things. This is where we can enhance our advantages to surpass AI. AI machines are syntactic and see the relationships among words, pictures, music, and video. They decode and encode the data and videos from one form to another (the T in GPT stands for transformer: Generative Pre-trained Transformer).

AI machines are currently challenged to find meaning behind actions or thoughts and to draw conclusions—that is, to make inferences. The machines are getting closer to emulating inferential thinking. As I write this book, OpenAI is moving its tech foundation to build reasoning engines with significant advancements in accuracy and self-checking reasoning capabilities. But they are still computational inference engines. This means that everything machines do is computing centered.

The AI Machines Are Catching Up

AI is moving incredibly fast. With the power of parallel computing, neural networks and algorithms will bring about brain-like intelligence. It will not be long before we will not be able to differentiate human intelligence from machine intelligence. Even though there are diverse ways to think—we humans make conclusions not just analytically but we also reason with emotion, gut feel, and other factors—we will not be able to differentiate human from machine intelligence.

Currently, Gen AI machines have yet to think for themselves. This will change as machines catch up with human reasoning. Machine inference and even machines thinking about thinking are becoming real. Today, they already sound human, they behave like people, and they are being treated like assistants who help us think. It's not a stretch to expect to see AI surpass human intelligence as we define it today.

We Still Have an Advantage—If We Work on It

As humans, we are able to create the future, not from the past but from our minds alone. We can form a future, informed by insight, hindsight, foresight, and eyesight, to will something into shape. Machines cannot achieve this, yet. Airbnb, Tesla, Uber, OpenAI, and NVIDIA join the list of unpredictable innovations, and leaders like Tom Cruise, Taylor Swift, Elon Musk, and Steve Jobs are category creators and join the list of unpredictable innovators. All of these innovative leaders display habits that support and encourage deep introspection at some time in their careers. Do you ever wonder whether AI machines can be introspective and are able to think about themselves or be reflective?

This is why we are so confused about AI and its implications for humans. The damn thing is smart but stupid at the same time. But it looks like it is gathering the world's knowledge and is going to eat our brains unless we do something.

Many books write about adapting to AI. Others write about abandoning AI. This book is about reclaiming our best innovative selves and dominating the AI relationship. This book is about what you and I can do to survive and grow our capabilities in an AI era.

We Humans MUST Surface Dormant Capabilities

We humans can create the yet-to-be-created. Machines create computational combinations that we may not see, but these combinations are still anchored in the information junkyard of our past. AI looks at what has already been done. Because AI taps into what humans have created, it is imprisoned by the past. But it can beat us on measures of intelligence like exams and tests. Sam Altman, founder of OpenAI, declared that although the new version was "not perfect," it had scored 90% in the United States on a bar exam and a near-perfect score on the high school SAT math test. It could also write computer code in most programming languages.[1] Oh dear. What do we do now!

My work has been about understanding what remains after AI machines copy/paste us. Is there nothing left? Or is there something that we possess that machines cannot manifest?

The Way Out Is In

We seem to seek a balance between humans and machines. Our ability to thrive in an unfamiliar environment depends on our ability to think innovatively and bring forward deep insights and to avoid relying exclusively on analytic-centered thinking machines. If we fail to do this, we fall victim to insight decay.

Insight decay is when we do not have any deeply nurtured ideas that are sparks in our mind. Research, which I explain in this book, suggests that our advantage over the machines comes from activating our minds beyond the limits of our brains. AI is computationally imitating the behavior of the brain, but our minds are not yet fully explored. In this book, we examine the difference between the mind and the brain. Trust that our minds are far more capable of seeing ahead and designing the future, whereas current AI machines help us computationally to understand the past.

I know my colleagues are concerned about AI. My lifelong research and professional journey have informed this book, and I seek to change your attitude toward AI from apprehension to inspiration. I hope that this book will shed a new light on the future of innovation and, most importantly, provide you with a way to develop your unique contribution to innovation in this AI world. Many people mistake creativity for being innovative. AI machines are displaying creativity and have shown incredible promise in their ability to create drawings and other artistic endeavors. Creativity is about thinking laterally and having ideas. Innovation is about taking these ideas, finding the insight in the idea, and building things people purchase and use commercially.

Our future is not assured, but it can be insured if we practice certain habits of the mind and behave in innovative ways instead of just following the norms of today. Build something with your innovative mind and use your creativity, then your cognitive capacity will live beyond AI.

This book presents a unique way to approach AI based on taking a deep look inside yourself. Here is a short guide to the chapters:

Introduction: The AI Era Awakens. Here I introduce you to AI and Gen AI, the new form of AI that is creating this new wave of productivity.

Chapter One: AI-Afraid, AI-Obsessed, or AI-Enabled? I discuss the three ways people are reacting to Gen AI. I explore what being obsessed with AI looks like and its long-term implications. This chapter is an introduction to what happens when we become obsessed with AI. We may experience cognitive atrophy.[2] If we think we are enhanced, we may rely on convenient paths while our brains atrophy. I focus on three behaviors that enable such decay.

Chapter Two: How to Be Insight-Centered and AI-Enabled. I open the conversation about the value of being insight-centered and what that looks like, especially with respect to AI. Here I address how to avoid the predicament of becoming obsessed with AI and thereby becoming insight-starved. I suggest that we should instead seek to become insight-centered and AI-enabled. I also explore the relationship between mind and brain.

Chapter Three: Are You AI Machine-Readable? Or Unreachable? If you are machine-readable, you might be replaced by next-generation AI machines. How do you become unreachable? What aspects of yourself do you develop?

Chapter Four: The Source of the Aha Moment! Insight is expressed in your mind as an aha moment. What is it, and how can one gain insight on demand? Is that even possible?

Chapter Five: The Inner Innovator: Be Machine-Unreachable. I dive into the details of what it means to be unreachable by AI machines. In this chapter, I review the research into our brain and mind's ability to leap beyond AI machines. This is what I call the inner innovator. If we innovate using our mind, we can become unreachable by AI. If we become machine-readable in our thinking and behavior, we are machine-replaceable.

Chapter Six: Unlocking Insight: The Sight of the Mind. I share the four sights of the mind and how insight is the superpower to develop.

Chapter Seven: Insight: Be Cause. I talk through one of the three ingredients that can create the conditions for insight to reveal itself. We explore the differences between taking a cause or being given a mission.

Chapter Eight: Insight: Configure Your Craft. Innovators must develop a unique craft that they can do better than others.

Chapter Nine: Insight: Unlock the Community. The third ingredient is collecting and identifying with a community rather than customers.

Chapter Ten: Build Scaffolding: The Language of Insight. Building a scaffolding holds the insight in place to launch. The first element of scaffolding is the use of transformative language.

Chapter Eleven: Build Scaffolding: Inspired Discipline. I address how one can inspire using a discipline approach to prototype your ideas, all in your mind first, then in the physical world.

In this book, I examine the richness of our cognitive selves so that you can manifest a recipe to dominate the future using, yet controlling, AI. You must choose to reclaim and operationalize your insights or be swept into the era of the AI-obsessed. When I use terms such as "Gen AI," I refer to new-generation chatbots, like ChatGPT, Gemini, or Claude, but I also include those technologies that are beyond chat, ones that function in the background to enable the machine intelligence. Further, when I refer to ChatGPT, know that I mean to represent the entire class of AI chatbots.

I honor the fact that Gen AI, the new form of AI, is lifting businesses and people to new heights of creativity, performance, and productivity. We can now paint, curate, author, and even produce music merely using "prompts" to these next-generation tools that are readily available to us. I think it is an amazing time to be alive with Gen AI. The challenge comes from the yet-to-happen side effects that result from the overreliance on and use of these strangely comfortable language interfaces (AI chatbots) that lull us into cognitive laziness, which leads to cognitive atrophy or decay.

There are ways out of this dilemma. I bring hope for us in the form of encouragement and ways to address our own ability to innovate, explore, and create insight beyond what is AI machine-readable.

Can Gen AI Make You Lose Your Mind?

When we become AI-obsessed and we give up thinking, we decay cognitively; hence, we lose our mind's essence. Although Gen AI is remarkably simple to engage with, asking it for assistance with every problem and embedding it in every productivity tool might be a Trojan horse that quietly drains our brains of critical thinking skills.

I am an advocate for the use of technology and AI to enhance our performance, our creativity, and more. But I also want to understand the cost. How can we train ourselves to not just respond to AI growth but to lead that growth by growing our own recipes of skills that make us unreachable?

I Prompt, Therefore I Am

René Descartes's famous theory, expressed in his Latin statement "cogito, ergo sum"[3] (I think, therefore I am), describes his foundational principle that if you doubt (and therefore think), the act of doubting proves your existence. AI has already challenged this foundational theory of existence. Descartes's focus was existence, not intelligence, because he based his theories of human existence on intelligent thought or doubt.

This is why I wrote this book with you, as an individual, as the focus and did not direct it to the business world around you. You are the center of excitement, doubt, and skepticism. You are the fundamental unit through which we can understand AI in our world. Are you confused about what Gen AI is doing to you? Are you having difficulty differentiating the hype from the real? Do you question our future with AI machines? Do you wonder what is going to happen to our younger generations who have absorbed all this assistance from Gen AI and are likely to end up insight-starved and AI-obsessed?

For these reasons, this book is directed to you, the individual. Many books talk about the corporate governance of AI or the technical approaches to AI and boardroom governance. I want to engage you as you engage AI and address how you grow and govern yourself.

Use It or Lose It

I argue that the "use it or lose it" principle applies to any muscle in your body. The brain, being the ultimate muscle, is subject to the same principle. If we let AI do the thinking and do not use this muscle and rely on AI, might we lose cognitive strength? On the other hand, might these thinking machines bring us to a higher level of cognitive capacity and intuition that we have yet to experience? This depends on our abilities to use it.

Some call AI the trigger for the fifth Industrial Revolution. But we, as humans, struggle to absorb even the implications of the fourth Industrial Revolution, let alone Gen AI.[4] In all other Industrial Revolutions, humans adapted and formed new ways to contribute to work. But the revolutions were around new sources of tools or energy to be employed. This GPT stuff is not a tool but a new species. This is more than a tool and might define a new way for us to be human. So, what happens to humans, and how do we evolve? What road map will show us the path to move beyond the AI machines and/or cooperate with them? What skills should we train ourselves in to be ready? Who must we become?

We humans have choices. Here is your first choice: Join me in this exploration. Join me as I discuss a framework for viewing the beauty and peril of Gen AI while we talk about what skills you must build. Let me offer a way to protect and grow your mind while enhancing your future productivity.

Let's explore ways to become innovators of our own destiny with Gen AI.

Introduction
The AI Era Awakens

In the eighties, I was fascinated by intelligent or cognitive databases that were designed and formed for machines to make intelligent decisions. It was a new field then, and my professor agreed that I should "read and review" several papers on the subject. I would labor over paper articles that I would discover in the University of Oregon library, consolidate all the writings into a cohesive report, and present my findings weekly to my professor. During those regular one-on-one meetings for my graduate work, I refined my premise that we would see a world beyond batch machines that used text as input, a world that would go beyond the models of interaction that existed then.

Our world was filled with batch machines that talked to us via punch cards fed into a machine so large we needed to have elevated floors that were air cooled. Hopefully, you can take yourself back in time to when icons, windows, desktop computers, microcomputers, visual screens, and Madonna had not entered our world. But, like Madonna, all of these technologies and personalities were simmering in the background.

At that time, we lived in a batch-processing world where users would punch decks of cards with their programming and then wait for a person who supported the machines in a closed, air-conditioned room. This attendant, who regularly wore a long white jacket like a medical doctor, would then take your deck and run it through the IBM 370 for you. They would then return the deck, the printout of your results, and a copy of your programming to you. If you could not work out an answer, you would have to do it all over again. Imagine the amount of time needed to create each punch card with your programming language punched into a machine language only the machine understood.

Then came the real-time machines—the DEC1099. They were smaller and clunky. You would work hunched over your machine, if you were lucky enough to get time on it, and you could get an almost immediate response to your work. Even then, those machines that we called interactive were responding in real time to code written on paper. Like an electric typewriter (which many of you have not used), it would accept the instructions we had typed onto a rolled paper and would respond with the energy of an old car, jumping around while hitting the paper with its levered characters, one at a time.

Real-time work was an advancement. Sometimes it would take hours of standing in line for a moment with the machine. So, you can imagine how crazy my proposals to my graduate school professor sounded. At the time, we had no user interface, no mouse, no interactive screen—only text input.

My research was on logical databases. I had seen enough research to understand that we could program machines to think and be almost human, but only if the data were organized to reflect the workings of our brains. At that time, we had algorithms that made machines almost human. But I also saw a whole new interface arriving, one that would be graphical, and I imagined that databases would be intelligent.

I proposed in my research that graphical user interfaces would exist to interrogate databases that had built-in intelligence. We could design systems that thought by themselves. That data had to be stored and retrieved in the same way our brains stored and retrieved information.

Much of my graduate research was based on the work done at Xerox PARC, the renowned lab in Palo Alto. Xerox PARC was the source of the mouse, as well as graphical interfaces (which Steve Jobs later copied). Their research papers defined the ideas that are now foundational to computing. Other sources were found under the term "logical databases."

Shortly after graduate school, I joined Intel to help with the propagation of the 80286 architectures. I still held on to the dream of user interfaces beyond text input and finding a way to capture and view data visually. I used my newly introduced microcomputer, the Intel 310, which took up almost half of my desk, to develop a few prototypes. In those days, microcomputers actually filled desktops. I was still dreaming of the way information should be presented to users, and I recall the computer fans keeping me warm while I worked many late nights at that cramped desk. The Windows architecture from Microsoft was just catching fire then. The internet and worldwide web were forming from ARPANET, and new machines were being introduced with the promise of a new era in computing.

I also became a writer about technology issues, which marked my start as an author. In 1984, I published my work on benchmarking in the then-popular magazine for computer enthusiasts called *BYTE*. That same issue introduced the first Macintosh—the first representation of the graphical, design-centered computer desktop. This computer had fonts and could draw beyond our wildest dreams. It had icons that collected information. It had a mouse! I remember the very day I saw a dream become an actual product. I cried with joy and some jealousy. I was excited about the future then. It was a time of immense possibilities.

Both of us, Steve Jobs and I, gained our inspiration from Xerox PARC, but one of us actually used his genius to develop the recipe that would change the world. I was excited for the possibility of the future of computing. The story goes that Steve Jobs took a tour of Xerox PARC and stumbled upon someone working on a new tool called a mouse and also saw how graphical user interfaces created a visual representation on screen. He rushed back to his office to create his vision, calling on his designers to build the first commercially workable mouse, and the genius of the Macintosh was born.

Today, with the new Gen AI as the catalyst, I feel like I felt years ago, when I worked in graduate school where everything was possible, knowing that new markets are forming. OpenAI and Google have awakened the world to the possibilities of Gen AI—they are the Xerox PARC of today. The transformation brought about by Gen AI is a watershed moment in human advancement. Unlike the Industrial Revolution that mechanized physical labor or the digital revolution that computerized information processing, the Gen AI revolution is fundamentally reshaping how we think and solve problems.

AI has been with us for almost fifty years as the science of AI, computer vision, and neural networks trying to imitate brain functions were developing. The development of high-powered computing platforms, like we have today, and the new discoveries of how to read unstructured data have sprung new innovations. Prior to Gen AI and large language models (LLMs), AI was using algorithms programmed to perform tasks and to review materials. Deep learning and neural networks existed, but the data had to be prepared, and the software had to be programmed to bring these frameworks alive. I use the term "AI" to speak of these technologies and principles that have brought us to this point. I use "Gen AI" to discuss the era that is now before us where AI machines can understand unstructured language, form their own generative conversations, and use deep learning to analyze the world's information.

The genesis of this new beginning can be traced to the development of the new transformer architecture in 2017 by Ashish Vaswani and colleagues at Google. Their seminal paper, "Attention Is All You Need,"[1] laid the groundwork for what would become a cascade of breakthroughs in artificial intelligence. The subsequent development of LLMs, beginning with GPT-3 by OpenAI in 2020, proved that these systems could exhibit sophisticated language understanding and generation capabilities that approached human-level performance in many tasks.

Subsequently, continued advancements have defied both the Turing test and Moore's law. The Turing test, designed by Alan Turing, the founder of modern computing, was a way to test whether a machine can behave in a human manner by placing a machine and a human in separate rooms while interrogating each. Until now, the Turing test would succeed because we could tell the difference. Now, we cannot discern the difference.

Moore's law, defined by Gordon Moore, cofounder of Intel, established the rule and predicted that the number of transistors on an integrated circuit would double every year for the next ten years, with his original paper published in 1965.[2] Why are these seemingly disconnected historical events important and connected now? Moore's law has become the benchmark for the growth rate of not just transistors but the growth of the technology computing industry as a whole. For decades we believed we were constrained by this law—until now. With Gen AI we are seeing exponential growth in computing and artificial intelligence. In fact, there is a belief that Moore's law has been shattered. This computing capacity never experienced before is now the basis of asking the Turing test question, which is whether we can discern a human interaction from a machine. Currently, the industry is failing the Turing test, namely that we are not able to discern a human from an AI machine, because our algorithms and computing power have reached escape velocity.

In healthcare, AI is already transforming patient care and medical research. Researchers have successfully employed deep learning to analyze complex medical records and assist in predicting hospital mortality, length of stay, and final discharge diagnosis. These models outperformed traditional models. And this was prior to Gen AI being invented. In drug discovery, companies have used AI to identify novel drug candidates for treating diseases like cancer and fibrosis, dramatically accelerating the traditional drug discovery pipeline from years to months.[3]

Education has seen equally dramatic changes. Early experiments have evolved into more sophisticated applications, with companies like Khan Academy integrating AI tutors that provide personalized learning experiences for millions of students worldwide. Sal Khan, its founder, has already created Khanmigo, a personal tutor that doesn't just provide an answer to students but uses queries to train the students to think for themselves.[4] OpenAI has introduced a new tool for students called "study mode"[5] in ChatGPT, which performs in similar ways to Khanmigo, using questions to teach students to learn.

McKinsey's recent paper titled "The Economic Potential of Gen AI," published in June 2023, provides insight into what Gen AI is contributing to our future. They believe it will add $2.6 trillion annually with sixty-three different use cases of applications and 75% of the financial impact in four areas, namely customer operations, marketing, sales, and software engineering. The impacted sectors are predicted to be banking, high tech, and life sciences.[6]

Most recently, the dream of self-driving cars, long confined to science fiction, has become a tangible reality. Companies like Tesla and Waymo expanded their testing of autonomous vehicles on public roads, showcasing AI's potential to revolutionize transportation. These AI-powered vehicles promise not only to reduce accidents caused by human error but also to reshape urban planning and reduce traffic congestion. There is also the question of what happens to Uber and Lyft drivers and the industry that has formed for workers who rely on this income. Nevertheless, we are moving headlong into self-driving cars and trucks and are now in a place where we are testing whether consumers will come along for the ride.

Beyond the roads, AI-driven drones have applications in various fields, from agriculture to emergency services. Farmers use autonomous drones for monitoring crop health using precision agriculture methods that are designed to evaluate the timing and style of care for crops.

From space to biology, Gen AI has accelerated outcomes because it is vastly efficient in digesting and isolating large datasets to find relationships and patterns, which humans cannot do in the same time frame. Drug research and discovery targeting illnesses like cancer have taken a leap as well.

DeepMind's AlphaFold has revolutionized protein structure prediction.[7] This achievement has accelerated research in fields ranging from drug development to environmental science.

Research at leading institutions like the Massachusetts Institute of Technology, Stanford, OpenAI, Microsoft, and Google suggest that we are only just beginning to scratch the surface of the Gen AI potential.

Children born today will grow up in a world where AI collaboration is as natural as using a smartphone is for current generations. The World Economic Forum projects that by 2035, most professional roles will involve some form of AI collaboration, fundamentally changing how we work, learn, and create.[8] This same study declared previously in 2023 that software engineering, UI/UX developers, and data scientists sat on top of the heap of those lucrative jobs needed. In just one year, those jobs are being replaced by AI machines.

The societal implications of this transformation are profound. While some jobs will be automated, new roles and industries will emerge. Workforces will have to be reskilled and transported to other jobs, and some, perhaps up to 75% of jobs today, will be handled by AI machines. This is according to the same McKinsey study I cited prior. I wrote this book to encourage us to rise to the transformation and not stay with the status quo. The book is about how Gen AI is growing and how we as humans can find the strength from within us to be insight-powered AI-enabled innovators who create the future yet to be experienced, led by Gen AI.

As we stand at the threshold of this new era, it's clear that Gen AI represents not just a technological revolution, but a fundamental shift in human capability. The challenge before us is to harness this technology in ways that enhance rather than diminish our humanity, that solve rather than create problems, and that bring us closer to rather than divide us from one another. For future generations, this technology will be as fundamental as electricity is today—an invisible but essential force that enables new forms of human creativity, discovery, and progress.

Gen AI is not going to leave. We must embrace it, learn about it, and explore it. If not, we will find ourselves at a disadvantage. Its use cases are varied, and it is important for us to ask how we humans should rise to be ready for this new species.

The dawn of an AI-enabled society had been long anticipated, but few could have predicted the rapid transformation that unfolded in the mid-2020s. As we stand in 2026, AI has woven itself into the fabric of our daily lives, reshaping industries, augmenting human capabilities, and opening new frontiers of innovation.

The potential for AI to enhance human capabilities, solve complex problems, and create a more efficient and personalized world is boundless. The key lies in harnessing this potential responsibly, ensuring that the benefits of AI are distributed equitably, and that the technology serves to augment, rather than replace, human ingenuity and creativity.

In this new era, the most successful individuals and organizations will be those who learn to collaborate effectively with AI, leveraging its strengths while keeping the uniquely human qualities that spur transformative innovation—that is, innovation to design and build the future yet to be imagined. As we look to the future, the promise of AI is not just in its ability to process data or automate tasks but in its potential to help us reimagine what it means to be human in an increasingly artificially intelligent world.

AI is here to stay. We must not fear it. We should act as explorers taking a journey of curiosity and understanding. But we also must bring our own critical insight to this change. We cannot wait until the dust settles. It will never settle. We must step up to become worthy of the future.

ACTION LEARNING

Journal your thoughts.

1. Be aware of AI and learn as much as you can about its implications.

_____

_____

_____

2. Use Gen AI tools and try to work with others who can guide you in your learning.

_____

_____

_____

3. Think like an explorer and innovator. Use your gut to feel and find your own path for your AI learning. Spend thirty minutes daily on any AI machine, testing out your understanding. Do not give it any information you feel is yours and private.

_____

_____

_____

4. Watch instructional videos on learning platforms like YouTube or others to pick up new ways to engage Gen AI.

_____

_____

_____

5. Insight is powered by inspiration. We discuss and explore this further in this book. What are your views about insight and inspiration in an Gen AI era?

_____

_____

_____

CHAPTER 1

AI-Afraid, AI-Obsessed, or AI-Enabled

We humans have taken readily to the technology found in the palms of our hands. The mobile phone is an addictive device we cannot live with or without. It is more intimate than our families and friends. Our phones know more about us and our habits than anyone. If your phone were to talk at your birthday, what would it tell the audience that they did not know?

To that end, we are now getting advanced cognitive capabilities in our phones. We are being watched and served at the same time. How are we to handle such a powerful second brain in our lives? It promises to elevate our capabilities, but it may also steal how we think because that's how it can help us more. But in that theft, do we permit cognitive liberties that decay our brain capacity?

I was leaving my hotel after a keynote recently, and I asked the bellhop for directions. He declared, "I don't have my phone with me. I can't tell you." In the world prior to mobile phones, the bellhop's primary job was to give us directions. But that job changed in the last ten years from providing directions to providing advice. In general, we don't need to use our own internal gyroscope because we have our computers for directions. We rely on words and speech from our phone that tell us to turn left and right. Like the bellhop, we use conveniently available technology to get from one place to the next. We have delegated our internal sense of direction to a machine. Will our brains shrink without use in the area of navigation when we overuse software tools for direction? Most likely! Consider research on London taxi drivers that analyzed how they engage driving and navigating using their grey matter posterior hippocampus, which is where we store our short- and long-term memories. This region was larger in drivers who navigated London streets than in those who did not use spatial navigation skills.[1]

As a former computer scientist, corporate executive, and entrepreneur, I am fascinated by the potential transformations Gen AI will enable in our future society and the productivity of our workforce. Yet, I am curious and cautious about its unplanned side effects on our thinking capacity, memory, and innovation.

How Do I Know If I'm AI-Obsessed?

Cocaine makes you believe that you are superhuman, even as it causes you to decay. It convinces you that more usage has exponential value. Are you caught in a similar delusion of productivity while experiencing cognitive atrophy from using Gen AI? Obsessing over AI is now evident in—but not yet fully infecting—our society. Consider the number of conferences, the funding principles in most venture capital funds, and the dinner table conversations about AI, and you clearly see a worldwide obsession over AI and its potential.

Before Gen AI, young people, who were forging ahead to explore the world and develop their own experiences, were acting on ideas originating from their minds. Today, many are first asking Gen AI for its opinion. What cognitive capabilities will be ill-formed as a result of the instantaneous use of this extended artificial brain?

The promise is clear. If you want to be a painter, writer, actor, script writer, or analyst, all you have to do is *pay and prompt*. Will we become accustomed to outsourcing our curiosity and cognitive capacity and abandoning the hard work that is designed to turn the raw mind and thoughts into meaning?

Facebook made us compare ourselves and boast. TikTok made us dance to others' tunes. Gen AI has the potential to be the ultimate cognitive drug of choice.[2] It can surround you with the world's knowledge and offer you the opportunity to check with it before you even begin to think or design.

In the same way, what becomes of us after years of simply prompting for our solutions but never really learning? Many people are using Gen AI technologies to learn to think differently and do what they could never imagine doing without help. Some are being artistic while others are writing no code but creating algorithms. This is magical. We live a paradox of a great opportunity for some and possible cognitive decay for others. Generally, people react in two ways to Gen AI. One is what I call AI-afraid, and the second is AI-obsessed. Both will create unwanted side effects in the future. The third, which I propose as the better way to react to Gen AI, is learning how to be AI-enabled (Figure 1). This book discusses the foundations of each of these responses and its impacts. Of course, I want you to choose AI-enabled.

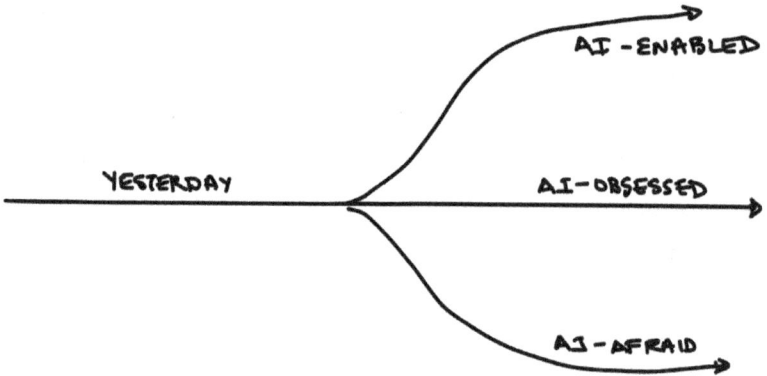

Figure 1. Pathways to Respond

Innovators can anticipate structural change and build the boat ahead of time to sail through the turmoil. This skill of seeing, anticipating, and innovating the ark before the flood is where humans beat AI. But one barrier clouds this inner sight in humans that machines do not have. Fear.

AI-FEAR

In "Fear Factor: Overcoming Human Barriers to Innovation,"[3] by McKinsey & Company, the authors declare that two factors differentiate leading innovator companies from those operating below average: culture and employee experience of innovation. The authors believe these factors correlate highly with success. They declare that fear is the constant factor—fear of a negative career impact, uncertainty, and loss of control. The authors call this the *ambiguity effect*. They also declare that such cognitive bias leads innovators within the organizations to avoid options with uncertain outcomes and seek predictable outcomes. Most of these attempts end up creating incremental changes rather than big changes to the status quo. In a study of more than one thousand participants, some laggards exhibited less experimentation and fewer ambiguous ideas.

Employees of top-performing companies were eleven times more likely to be incentivized to take risks and five times more likely to report being encouraged to experiment.

Fear seems to be a constant. The essence of the McKinsey study is that corporations have collective fear now more than ever. Fear expresses itself when we constantly question our decisions, when we burn out, when we develop unproductive objectives to "cover our ass," and in many more behaviors. Fear is the underlying factor that determines or encourages our inertia or momentum. Notably, the authors do not state that companies who enhance innovation remove fear. Instead, they have systems that compensate for it. Are you afraid, or are you excited? Many believe fear is overcome by courage. But in business, we cannot set up systems where courage is designed to overcome fear. It cannot work. We need a more structured approach to fear management.

Inspiration compels us to act and creates an immunity to fear. The movies we watch tell the wrong story, in which the hero is first a coward and then suddenly reaches a boiling point, bringing out courage. We celebrate our $16 movie ticket purchase, even though it is unreal.

Although courage overcomes fear, it is not compelling enough to drive innovators. Inspiration, on the other hand, propels us to recognize fear and build mental fortresses that withstand it.

Why am I harping on fear? I am starting with it because without understanding that fear is ever present, we will hide under it, waiting for some energy from outside to help us. Consider counteracting fear with something greater and more compelling that takes us to another place: inspired thought and action. AI is a wonderful innovation that has applications in everything we do. It can take us to a new dimension if we can overcome our fear of it and figure out how to harness it.

AI-OBSESSED

AI-obsession is an overreliance on and indulgence in Gen AI. I know of users who rely on Gen AI for almost everything they question or are in doubt over. One person responds via text to blind dates using AI chatbots, placing all the text responses into the AI tech and asking for how to respond. I know of others who decide their day's planning and even clothing based on AI. Then there are those who seek advice on divorce, dating, and even social issues. Of course, chatbots help when it comes to running meetings, being extroverted, or writing that carefully worded funeral message. But many ask chatbots to think for them before they think for themselves. It seems so much more convenient. Over time, three human tendencies can exaggerate our overreliance on AI and, possibly, cause cognitive decay or atrophy:

1. The curse of convenience
2. The temptation of good enough
3. The loss of the right to one's own first opinion

THE CURSE OF CONVENIENCE

Does Gen AI increase your cognitive capacity, or does it deprive you of the training you need for the future? Does the convenience of asking your chatbot what to make for dinner or how to decide on a trip itinerary overcome the concern that you may give up thinking?

Are you off-loading your important learning functions under the guise of convenience, and does this mean you will find yourself cognitively decayed later in your life? Or is Gen AI going to increase and enhance your cognitive self to levels yet to be understood or anticipated? When I am on panels at conferences, there is always one panelist who will look sideways at me and say, "We felt the same way about the calculator. We said it would kill our brains. It did not." They are correct. But keyboard typing killed handwriting. Looking at screens killed human connections. So, what happens when Gen AI enters our minds?

A study done at the Swiss Business School's Center for Strategic Corporate Foresight and Sustainability focused on the use of Gen AI tools and critical thinking. They also examined the impact of cognitive off-loading to AI tools on critical thinking. They found that higher Gen AI usage correlated with reduced critical thinking. As cognitive off-loading to Gen AI increased, critical thinking scores decreased. Of the more than six hundred respondents, the younger subjects displayed higher Gen AI usage, greater cognitive off-loading, and lower critical thinking scores. The study also noted a correlation between levels of education and off-loading.[4] Here, the more educated, the less off-loading. This implies that the younger and lesser educated will off-load more and possibly experience cognitive atrophy.

We love convenience. But convenience, before we know what we are outsourcing, could dull our own mental skills. To use Gen AI well, do not allow yourself to take the easy road. Do not just ask Gen AI everything without learning from it. In the chapters that follow, I explain how inconvenient learning or trial and error actually builds your brain. This means that the convenience of over-using Gen AI dulls your brain in the long run.

THE TEMPTATION OF GOOD ENOUGH

As a musician, I used to be able to detect whether any music played was machine-generated or created by studio machines, and I refused to appreciate machine-generated music. Today, I'm bopping my head to drum machines and synthetic music with auto-tuned singers! What has changed in me? Remember Milli Vanilli, the breakout duo from the UK that was discovered to be lip syncing and did not write their own songs? Prior to the scandal, they received a Grammy award in the nineties. They sold about thirty million singles. The duo was a creation of manager Frank Farian, who found studio musicians to sing on the tracks while the duo toured worldwide just lip syncing. In July 1989, in an MTV performance, the hard drive malfunctioned, skipping through the song. But even after that, they performed, and the audience did not care. Only after individual backup singers objected did the false story crumble under the weight of the truth. The point of this story is not the crime—it's that the audience did not care. The act was good enough.

Many of my colleagues are okay with computer-generated essays, poems, marketing analysis, or even machine-generated paintings. The general audience has lowered its need for originality, authenticity, or above-average work with the curse of good enough. And so have I.

Many Gen AI-augmented posts, write-ups, and marketing plans are boringly the same—they revert to the mean. Until I realized that good enough was eroding my cognitive advantage, I accepted good enough. Now it is not enough. Set your standards above just good enough and reach for the extraordinary. Strive, and your brain will thrive.

LOSING YOUR FIRST OPINION RIGHTS

Are you becoming an editor of machine-generated ideas or the originator of your thoughts? We started with the assumption that Gen AI will help us by being our copilot or agent. We can produce more and exponentially scale ourselves. We now realize that Gen AI and GPT technology can offer imaginative ideas, draw for us, paint posters for us, and even write for us. We are now asking the machines for their first opinion, which leaves us to respond rather than create. In the past, the first opinion was always assigned to the owner of our creativity and cognition—our brains. Many Gen AI habitual users contend that they get more ideas to start their thinking using Gen AI. But when we become editors rather than creators, what happens to our cognitive originality? Where can we find lasting advantage as machines grow in computational strength and we weaken in our cognitive origination?

Many young people ask the machine for ideas to trigger their research papers or even their emails to each other. This weakens their ability as members of a human society to form the first opinion and take the cognitive energy to create original thoughts. When they start any project challenge, their first thought is to ask Gen AI to help launch their thinking. We should try to avoid using it to start thinking. If not, the Gen AI machines will drive our thinking, and they will generally bring us down to the mean or the average of what they know.

The Google Effect—I Google, Therefore I Am

We have already given up remembering items if we know where we stored them. It's called the "Google effect."[5] Professor Betsy Sparrow, at Columbia University, studied this phenomenon where we are less prone to remember items that we know we can retrieve, and we remember where we left it more than the facts themselves. What happens when we off-load our thinking? These experiments revealed that we are prone to search for information and remember where this information resides versus the actual details of the information. What if you are provided the answers to your questions, as in ChatGPT or other Gen AI tools? Will we stop thinking and know only how to prompt a Gen AI engine?

The future seems so bright, and we must welcome Gen AI to spur our innovative spirit. Many ask whether we should dive into this Gen AI pool. This is a logical question, but it is the wrong question. We stare at the pool in front of us, when behind us looms a Gen AI tsunami readying itself. The pool symbolizes a spot for us to dive into the narrative. We have no choice. Inevitably, the Gen AI tsunami will reach us and take over our lives.

Currently, we are "hiring" Gen AI for the jobs to be done.[6] We give it our data and prompt it to generate a way of thinking. We provide all of our creativity and the expressions of our world, our paintings, our writings, our programming, and our music. In the pre-Gen AI (I call this AI in the book) era, we created algorithms, set rules, and input data for the machine to analyze. We also pushed the boundaries of technology with machine-learning algorithms that tried to imitate the human brain. With Gen AI, we and our outputs are the data for the AI machine to ingest. In a strange way, in current times, Gen AI hires us to understand us better. It may be eating our brain to understand how it can help us.

It's so convenient to not think and ask a machine to think for us. But, someday, the machine may decide we are an inconvenience. This seems dystopian, yet without this consideration, we will become complacent, accepting every offer of convenience as a productivity advance that enhances our lives.

Consider this: We used to be directionally capable. We used maps and our internal compass. Today, after living with mobile phones that provide directions, we are unable to find our way around as we used to. Our internal gyroscope or compass, found within our brain, has atrophied, and frankly, we seldom miss it. Research[7] has isolated this compass, which coordinates our sight and our sense of location within our brain. This cognitive off-loading might reduce our ability to develop and follow directions unless we practice using our internal maps. I practice both internal and external off-loading just to keep up in this data-obese world. I point at something I want to remember (internal), or I write things down or store it in my phone to remember (external).

Let's return to the question of "Should we adopt AI or wait?" Well, it is too late. Gen AI will be everywhere, whether you choose it or not. Software companies are delivering Gen AI through existing software you are familiar with. You will find it with general tools like

Microsoft Word and other applications as well as apps that manage your photographs. Today, it writes software. It connects applications to complete any task you wish, which you command with your voice. We call these Agentic AI, where we can instruct the AI machines to execute pre-formed tasks for us.

Gen AI will appear in your stream of apps at work and home before you realize it. And it will help you do your work better and faster and without hesitation. Compared with 2023, respondents of the 2024 survey by McKinsey stated that they are much more likely to be using Gen AI at work and even more likely to be using Gen AI both at work and in their personal lives.[8] One small section in this report about business usage of Gen AI highlighted an above-normal rise of personal use between 2023 and 2024. This is all done in search of convenience. People are using Gen AI increasingly in the privacy of their homes.

How to Be AI-Enabled

It would be ironic if all we have to do to be AI-enabled is to do the opposite of AI-obsessed behaviors. That would make a short book! Apart from decreasing your AI-obsessive tendencies, the research and my practical experiences and those of others point to three behaviors that are foundational to AI-enablement. The three ways to counteract obsessive AI impacts are listed next and shown in Figure 2:

1. Create the habit of experimentation.

2. Use Gen AI as your second opinion, not the first.

3. Reclaim your ability to gain insight, your aha!

AI - OBSESSED

Follow convenience

Gen AI as 1st opinion

Settle for good enough

⇩

COGNITIVE ATROPHY

AI - ENABLED

Pursue Experimentation

You as 1st opinion, Gen AI as editor

Reclaim your insight (aha!)

⇧

INSIGHT ENHANCEMENT

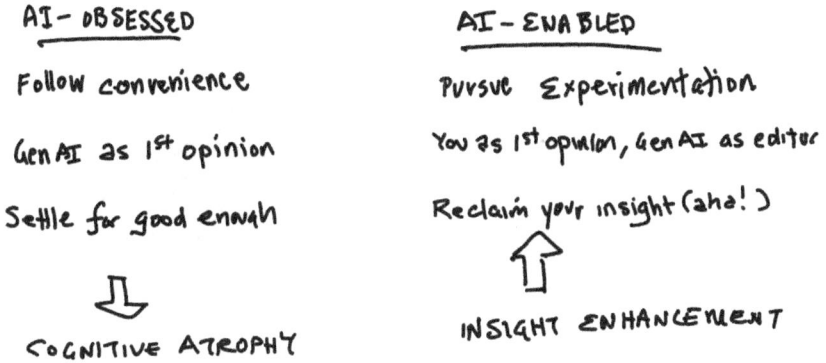

Figure 2. AI-Obsession vs. AI-Enablement Behaviors

In a sense, you are your own LLM filled with experiences, notions, instincts, and facts. Prompting yourself instead of the AI machine will train and retrain your cognition to be an active participant. The rest of this book discusses these concepts. But, to satisfy the insatiable curiosity for answers to this challenge, let me elaborate on the first and second items in the previous list.

First, keep trying and experimenting with anything difficult to solve. Keep trying until you get tired of failing. This is the exercise of your insightful mind. It loves to fail and try again, and every time you do, it is growing its cognitive strength. In a way, you must earn the right to get that aha. But to do that, experiments are good. Fearless failure is good.

Second, the following research will show that starting with your opinion or ideas helps you remember, store, and act on those ideas better than if a machine provided the framework or the idea. Many of my colleagues love GPT because it gives them the first start to think through stuff. Well, just as we love someone to get the work done for us, we think we are expedient or even successful. We are neither. In fact, it's a recipe for cognitive atrophy. So, start an endeavor with the struggle for your opinion first. This takes research, experience gathering, determination, repeated trials, and failures with no promise of a successful outcome. But what that does to your brain is miraculous. It builds its cognitive connections and mass. Idle minds that skip this step create unused capacity that, after some time, cannot return.

So skip the stage of asking your favorite GPT to start you off with ideas. Skip the open-ended prompt that asks the machine to guide when you have yet to think through a direction. I believe it's more than okay to ask it to teach you as an expert on a topic so that you can understand, learn, and empower your ideas, but when you creep across that unseen line to asking it to tell you, then you are giving the rights to your own first opinion to a mindless machine that has been trained to respond based on the collective data it has been trained on.

I am proposing that there are three ways of not being obsessed with AI, and giving your own exploratory self away because of obsessive use of Gen AI can cause an atrophy in the number of insights (aha moments) you receive in the future. In a sense, you approach being data-obese and insight-starved. Here you know a lot of information, can find it fast, and explain it, but cannot see how your story weaves and guides these random pieces of information to form insight.

Why Is Insight so Important?

Insight is the foundation of how innovators differ from intelligent machines. It is also how transformational innovators differ from those who seek incremental improvements or to maintain the status quo. Transformational insight is part of a family of "sights" that I call the sights of our mind. A subsequent chapter discusses these four sights of the mind. Can we produce insight when we want to? I say yes. But we must subdue our brain's habit of consuming information in order to let our mind bloom. If not, we decay as we push more information into our brains while AI machines do our thinking for us. What I mean is that we need to train our minds to innovate and to be inspired by transformational insights.

How Do You Know You Are Having an Original Thought?

Have you ever confidently shared a "fact" you swore you have known forever, only to realize you Googled it moments ago? Turns out, this digital amnesia is reshaping our understanding of knowledge itself.

One study[9] observed the effects on memory of cognitive off-loading. This is when people rely on external devices for their thinking. In this research with 172 candidates, researchers found candidates in the test were very effective in test performance using off-loading but did not remember the subject matter compared to those who did not off-load.

Another fascinating study,[10] this one by Adrian F. Ward, explored this phenomenon and involved nearly two thousand participants across eight experiments. The results are pretty eye-opening—when people use Google to find information, they have a hard time distinguishing between what they actually remember and what they just found online. It's like our brains are treating Google as an extension of our own memory. The internet acts as a powerful external memory source, and because it's so seamlessly integrated into our cognitive processes, we often can't tell where our internal knowledge ends and the internet's knowledge begins. It's almost like we're outsourcing our memory to the internet without even realizing it.

The study found that people who used Google not only answered more questions correctly, they also felt more confident in their cognitive abilities. They predicted they would perform better on future tests, even without internet assistance. It's like they were attributing the knowledge they found online to their own internal smarts. The researchers found that this overconfidence can have significant cognitive consequences when the internet isn't available.

Suddenly, all that knowledge we thought we had disappears with our dropped Wi-Fi connection. It's like we're building a house of cards with our knowledge, and Google is the foundation. Pull it away, and everything comes tumbling down. The study found that the rapid delivery of information from search engines like Google can actually make this misattribution worse. When we get information so quickly, we don't have time to reflect on our own knowledge limitations. It's almost like the information bypasses our usual cognitive checkpoints.

A more recent study, performed at MIT Media Labs, led by Nataliya Kosmyna, PhD, focused on the impacts and cognitive cost of using an LLM in the context of writing an essay.[11] Candidates were separated into three groups: an LLM group, a search engine group, and a brain-only group (54 total participants). Using EEG to record their brain activity, the researchers tried to understand how writing an essay would affect the brain in these three circumstances. The essays would also be analyzed by human reviewers. The results (note that the sample size is small) showed that the brain-only group had the strongest network activation in the brain. The search engine usage team showed intermediate engagement, while the LLM team showed the least level of cognitive engagement. Of course, these experiments applied only to writing, but in this we find many nuances that the study focuses on. For our purposes, this study does show that the use of search engines is less impactful than the use of LLMs to write an essay.

Save Your Brain by Understanding Your Limits Before Using Gen AI

In the previously mentioned experiments by Adrian Ward, the fifth experiment involved researchers asking participants to write down their answers before consulting Google. Guess what happened? By forcing people to confront their own knowledge first, it helped them understand their limitations better. The respondents showed lower confidence in their internal knowledge after this exercise. It's like making people do a knowledge inventory before they start borrowing from Google's vast library. It is almost like creating a mental buffer between our curiosity and our Google reflex. The researchers also tried delaying the search results to see what would happen. And as you might guess, that also helped reduce the misattribution. By slowing down the process, people had more time to recognize that they were relying on external information rather than their own knowledge.

It's fascinating how just a small delay can make such a big difference in our cognitive processes. This phenomenon could affect how we construct and understand knowledge in our society as a whole. If we're all walking around thinking we know more than we do, it could lead to a false sense of expertise across the board. It's like we're building a society on a foundation of Google searches that we've mistaken for genuine understanding.

In another experiment by Adrian Ward, he found that this misattribution effect is particularly pronounced when we're dealing with questions of moderate difficulty. It's like there's a sweet spot where we feel like we should know the answer, but we don't quite have it at our fingertips. That's when we're most likely to confuse Google's knowledge with our own. When something is really easy, we know we know it. And when something is super difficult, we're aware that we're learning new information. But it's that middle ground where things get tricky. It's like our brains are primed to say, "Oh yeah, I knew that!" when in reality, we just learned it from Google a moment ago.

Here's another interesting tidbit from the research. This effect seems to be strongest right after we've looked something up. Over time, our confidence in our own knowledge tends to decrease. If you quiz yourself a day or two after Googling something, you're more likely to accurately assess what you actually know. It's about developing the metacognitive[12] skills to understand the limits of our own knowledge and being aware of how we think. Schools might need to incorporate exercises that help students distinguish between what they truly know and what they can quickly look up. It's about teaching students to be humble and curious learners rather than overconfident Google-assisted experts.

The first thing we can do to counteract this effect is to pause and reflect before we search for information. We should ask ourselves what we actually know about this topic. This creates a mental buffer between our curiosity and our Google reflex. And when we do look something up, we can be more conscious of the fact that we're accessing external information. Maybe even say it out loud: "I'm looking this up because I don't know it."

Another strategy is to challenge ourselves to explain concepts in our own words after looking them up. If we can't do it, it's a good sign that we haven't really internalized the information yet. It's about developing a healthier relationship with the vast amount of information at our fingertips.

Now, take this research and replace "Google search" with Gen AI. What do you think the results would show? We have limited research yet on such impacts. But I theorize that users will believe themselves more intelligent, better writers, and better musicians or poets.

Are Gen AI solutions addictive and eating your brain? Has cognitive theft already begun? Under the "cloud" of understanding you to serve you, these machines are collecting and emulating not just what you want but how you think about what you want. If we will not differentiate what we know versus what we find, we had better understand our own limits and the gaps in our knowledge before we use Gen AI. Most of the rest of the book discusses how to avoid AI-obsession and be AI-enabled, but we also explore the potential of our mind and how we can utilize it to bring forth a worthwhile recipe to be innovative in a world filled with present-day followers.

Machines do not sleep, so they cannot dream. Humans dream. Machines cannot take an idea and build mental scaffolding for others to build, climb, and become innovators. Humans can.

As I prepared for this book, I realized that I write to learn. So, what have I learned?

1. Gen AI is everything to a few people. But it is confusing to the rest.

2. The famous quote "AI won't replace humans—but humans with AI will replace humans without AI"[13] is not correct. Obsessive use of Gen AI can decay your brain. So, only humans who use Gen AI with an eye to obsession or enablement have an advantage.

3. Gen AI is not static and is growing faster than humans are. Humans must step up.

4. Humans are generally convenience seekers, and this characteristic may destroy our cognitive capacity or, at minimum, alter our cognitive growth.

5. A new species has entered our world. For us to partner with this new species, we must do more than learn AI, we must learn new skills to dominate in our own way. We must be explorers as well as innovators. Given that the new world is unknown, innovating without exploring will not suffice.

6. We have a great opportunity to be unimaginably successful if we know what skills are needed and how to enhance them.

ACTION LEARNING

Journal your thoughts.

1. Know that what you put into a machine is no longer yours. It belongs to the world.

_____

_____

_____

2. Your algorithm of life is yours. It took you years to build. Explore what your thinking and innovating processes are and protect them well.

_____

_____

_____

3. Know that you are beyond the machine. You are a biological and psychological recipe with instinct and experience at gathering multi-generational insights. Some of your insights will be biased. Others will be protective. But those deeply rooted insights into the future will be an advantage that machines do not possess. Machines cannot create original thought. They are amazing at combining existing documented thoughts to create unique solutions. Drug discovery is one example as the machines can look at all the research and find new drug therapies founded on existing work and research. Gen AI machines are trained on a collection of past expressions, such as writings, photos, and videos. You are a collection of experiences and wisdom that creates insight. As I formulate these observations, through explorations, with you, I have placed these explorations in this book. Join me.

_____

_____

_____

4. What is your greatest concern about how Gen AI will impact you?

_____

_____

_____

5. How do you prepare your mind for this concern?
List ALL the ways.

_____

_____

_____

6. What is your greatest excitement about Gen AI and you?

_____

_____

_____

7. How do you prepare your mind to capture this opportunity?
List ALL the ways.

_____

_____

_____

CHAPTER 2

How to Be Insight-Centered and AI-Enabled

By the time this book is published, Google's NotebookLM will be more advanced in features than it is now. If you do not know what NotebookLM does, it takes any input from text or videos and creates a podcast conversation between two machine-generated avatars, usually one who sounds male and one who sounds female. They discuss the topic you have injected into NotebookLM, and the output is a fully developed conversation in almost real time. If you listen to the avatars, they interrupt each other, are humorous, speak in metaphors, and conduct insightful conversations like humans. This is a shocking idea. How did this idea actually take form? What is the story of such an amazing invention?

Meet Raiza Martin, product leader at NotebookLM, which was incubated at Google Labs. The Gen AI-generated podcasts she and her team create are very relatable and are not like machine-generated results. It all started as a Google 20% project for Raiza. Raiza was leading a Gen AI Test Kitchen[1] project, and she remembers she raved about cool ways to use audio. At first, it was Raiza and an engineer, and then others joined later. One engineer and Raiza!

NotebookLM was first launched as a chat interface. Gemini came out around the same time. Audio models were available inside the labs. They would generate a surprise of sorts when you uploaded a resume, for example, transforming it into a podcast.

Raiza started from the problem rather than from a lab model where you start with the technology. The audio feature existed in the lab already. Raiza was interested in voice input and output. The team thought about how to make the audio feature cool.

Raiza talks of shaping tech to get it closer to people. The secret sauce behind this is called the content studio. The genius of her idea lies in asking how to shape the audio. She notes that Usama Bin Shafqat, the engineer, is the craft person who brings out the best of the audio. The electronic hosts laugh, talk, joke, and have a human time. How?

A content studio is technology that works on top of the LLM. Raiza had to do a lot of listening as quality assurance to know how to present this to the world. Raiza would listen to audio overviews over and over again at her home. Her husband, who did not know that she was listening to Gen AI-created conversations, wondered what she was listening to. He assumed they were real podcasts. Googlers now upload their group check-in updates of what they have achieved, using this feature to explain their work. Raiza, Usama, and others had found a new way to touch customers directly and operate differently.

Raiza came from startups and designed and built software for electronic payments. When she joined her favorite boss at Google, she was excited to go from 0 to 1 again, that is, to start from nothing and build something The lab moved fast because everything was done in parallel, not linearly like all other parts of Google.[2]

But what has this insight-centered creation, NotebookLM, transformed? Researchers can input a detailed research paper and tell NotebookLM what to concentrate on as the premise, read other research papers, and synthesize these seemingly disjointed papers into a thoughtful analysis comparing and contrasting them. Your work no longer needs to be sequential. Nor does it need to take much time.

How about videos? Video viewers can place them all into NotebookLM, and the output is a podcast conversation that finds connections that take days or months to find among the videos. You don't need to view ten videos to uncover synchronous messages or even connect the dots. Just listen to one podcast. Students are using this feature to understand complex and large volumes of textbooks this way.

Like Raiza and her team, we must step ourselves up to a much higher level than simply being editor or prompter. Humans must become explorers who innovate beyond the prompted suggestions of their machines. We must see beyond the past that has been reconfigured and retrofitted to the future. In order to take our place next to AI machines, we must become golden egg makers. In this new world of Gen AI, we must learn to be inner innovators like Raiza and Usama. Learn and retrain yourself to ingest and expel transformative insights and build them. Inner innovators, like Raiza, get aha moments and create the future and bring it to the present.

Many users of Gen AI are obsessed with its capabilities and are forgoing their own insights—but those insights are derived from the machines they use. They have yet to train their minds to be insightful, that is, to see through to their ever-changing future. They continue to give their machines everything they are questioning, and the machines produce outputs that, to them, seem to be original works. They don't realize the machine is producing outputs based on pure pre-trained deliverables. The machines are combining what they have been trained to understand and computationally providing that to you. Inner innovators, like Usama, study and explore Gen AI and then create new ideas using it as a foundation to build the yet-to-be-imagined future.

Using Your Mind Is Different than Using Your Brain

I coined the phrase "how not to lose your mind" as a way to say that your brain does not define you. Your mind does. *Unreachable* is about you seeing that misfocusing on how to master your brain using AI will not help you find the real truths and capabilities that lie in your mind. I define the mind to be not the muscle we hold in our head, but the entire system of our intelligence we carry in our nervous system, our brain, our senses, our spinal cord, and our gut. Computer scientists have, very effectively, emulated our brain's functional capabilities using neural network technology. We have become so enamored with how our neurons are connected that we have neglected the vastness of our minds,[3] which has far more potential to impact our intelligence. We have interpreted intelligence as a machine emulating our sight, a portion of our brain, and data crunching. There is more to intelligence than what is being captured by current Gen AI.

A powerful philosophical discussion of the brain–mind relationship can be found in a paper titled "A Neurologist Looks at Mind and Brain: 'The Enchanted Loom,'" by Phiroze Hansotia.[4] Here he highlights the various views and perspectives of the brain–mind debate. Our mind involves deeper understandings found in our nervous system, our brain, our senses, and our DNA of experiences that collectively provide us with insights.

The brain is a filter for your thinking while the mind creates thoughts. The brain is the muscle in your head that is the world of neurons and connections. The mind is the extended brain that includes the body's intelligence, the sense intelligence, the wisdom in your cells, and your history of interpreted experiences. AI machines are not generating thoughts, they are imitating the generation of thoughts, organizing words, and putting the words together that can simulate thinking. Someday, and very soon, inference engines will create and own their own thinking. Today, inference engines follow and imitate what we program them to think and do. Once inference engines become widespread and even machines that introspect—that is, think about thinking—are prevalent, our world will become even more transformative. Intelligence is the product of the brain. In contrast, insight is the sight of the mind.

Many leaders are unable to define the future when most of the future is unclear and challenged by new variables; the future seems filled with the fog of the unknown unknowns. We cannot see what new structural changes come at what size and what likelihood. Yet, some innovators avoid predicting the future by creating the future they imagine. Explore and look into this unseen future and see through the fog by using the sight of your mind. Begin to learn and experiment.

Don't just learn everything you want about AI or ask AI what it thinks the future holds. That is valuable but not what you must discover. You must explore how to learn, experiment, and gain experience. Prepare not just your brain but your mind, which can travel to places machines have yet to go; your mind will be guided by your insights derived from your physical, emotional, and symbolic experiences.

I held a strategy meeting with a large corporation that wanted us to review all their market research, information, and stats prior to our session. I insisted they did not want that. I refused all such business analysis because I knew that what they had gathered, their competitors had also gathered. It was merely documenting the past. I asked these executives to walk into the strategy session with the power of their own intellect, drawing on the full force of what they had captured their entire life. It was magical what happened in those sessions when humans relied on their own wisdom. After two days, we found our focus and our strategy and then tested it with the available data.

In your brain, you are building a database of high-resolution views, impressions, and rules. This is what the machine is trying to imitate and scale. But your mind holds untold mysteries ready to await your requests for insight.

Being Information-Obese Makes You Insight-Starved

If you stuff your brain with facts and figures, your mind may lose its ability to generate insights. The following chapters present the research on this topic. Your brain loves data, and your mind loves stories. But training your mind to do both is what raises your capability above Gen AI. Everyone consumes information, even when we resist. Carrying a heavier bag of information does not give you an advantage. Machines will carry this for you. Loosen your hold on information and grab lightly on to insight-generating conditions. Identify the circumstances in which you generate insights and then apply those insights often. Build that practice with your mind, not your brain.

Have you ever been to a party where you can guess what the topics of discussion will be? Most parties fit that description. It's always what they saw on YouTube, the recent elections, the common news, or Saturday Night Live jokes. The conversation consists of common intelligence and common ignorance and is insight-starved and information-obese. Some conversations lack deep insightful appreciations. Many lack anything but information strung together in quotable quotes that were discovered many times over. Pack your brain, and your mind will lose insight. Information is already present and is the junkyard of the past when it arrives.

Insight—the Sight of the Mind

The wisdom inside you, insight, is seldom a gift; rather, it is earned with practice. In common terms, insight is expressed as an aha moment. Aha moments are seemingly sudden but are nuanced in their origins in our brains and minds. In fact, their origins are still mysterious. Aha moments take practice and inspiration to trigger. It takes work and experience to refine your plans and intentions to innovate.

Malcolm Gladwell speaks of ten thousand hours or ten years in his book *Outliers*, a careful study of how normal leaders become exceptional icons. I believe that after that hard work of the ten thousand hours of practice, you can reach a state of mind that generates a new way to look at this world using insight. Your innovator mind needs fuel to launch ideas. Insight is that fuel, and you can see it in your own wisdom, if it is protected from external noise.

When you gain an insight, you are capable of redefining what you witness in new ways. People often mistake insight for inspiration. Inspiration is an emotional flint that moves you to act upon experiences you witness. Inspiration is usually from the outside world that you gain an internal insight about. With insight, you see the future in your mind. You are then inspired to act upon that insight.

I asked Dr. Naomi Fried, CEO and founder of PharmStars and managing partner of PharmStars Venture fund, how she decided to start her company. She lit up and spoke without hesitation, saying that she awakened in the middle of the night with the entire structure and purpose of the company and could not stop until she created that which the dream awakened. Missions are given to you, but causes are taken by you. You are never the same when you pick up a cause greater than yourself.

Julie Sweet, CEO of Accenture, speaks of reskilling workers in a unique way. Of course, Gen AI is disrupting all work and replacing more than reskilling us all. Julie seeks learners and leaders in how she looks for talent.[5] She frames the question to interview candidates as: What did you learn in the last six months? She is not picky about what, only that they are exploring. If they are not learning and being a leader of their own environment, she would be less interested. This strikes at the heart of the new skills required beyond AI—next generation leaders who can lead in multidimensional ways, not just using technology but moving humans forward and having a learning mindset.

Eyesight, foresight, and hindsight come from the brain. Eyesight is what you see before you. Foresight is what your brain tells you will come in the future. Hindsight is what you interpret as having happened prior to this moment. Gen AI does tell you what's present; it articulates possible scenarios for the future based on data it has collected about the topic you discuss and gives you the history you ask for. It is limited to the language, videos, and voices it has swallowed and been trained on. That is fantastic when the world of the future is a projection of the past.

When you concentrate on being more informed, you pack your brain with the know-how needed to communicate using promptable AI machines. You also pack your brain with more analytics and deconstructive thoughts on past data. The more you deceive yourself and tell yourself that you are rationally at an advantage over the machines, the more likely it is that the irrational, instinctive, unstructured pathology of the future may overcome you. You cannot run forward looking backward, unless your world is predictable and stable, in which case you can close your eyes and run while basing your insights on historical computations.

Those who master creativity, insight generation, cause-driven inspiration, and unique approaches to product- and solution-making might just win over the attention of the markets and differentiate themselves over the AI-obsessed humans who believe they are augmented by machines.

Any study of innovative leaders shows that those with insight can bend reality, see the future as their own vision, and form new markets. These are the ones we remember. From Jeff Bezos to Steve Jobs, from Gandhi to Mother Teresa, we find generators of transformative outcomes. These leaders have changed our lives through their use of insight, not found in the common thinking, and by building the scaffolding that allows us to climb and transform our lives. But this thing we call the mind is different than what machine learning and GPT/Gen AI is imitating and seems to enable. What Gen AI gives us is the integrated and documented record of our innovative past, all our expressions of ourselves in words, pictures, videos, and websites, organized to power the future.

The origins of thoughts and ideas are still not understood or documented. Our minds are where we manufacture insight, the aha, the wisdom from our cognitive foundation, our experience, and the deep heritage of our genetics.

Status Quo and Transformative Innovators

AI is hyper useful to optimize the status quo that wants to preserve and improve the current ways of doing and being. The innovator wants to challenge the current status quo. Status quo sees history as a guide; the transformational innovator wants to make history. Status quo sees top-down rules; the innovator wants to develop from within themselves, where ideas live. Status quo leaders will remove the unmeasurable to gain speed and efficiency advantage; innovators embrace the intangible because there lie the nuances of the future. Status quo leaders start with investigation because life to them is rational and predictable; innovators seek inspiration first. Status quo likes money or mission as measures; innovators seek meaning and future relevance first and then money.

This battle between status quo thinking and transformative

innovative thinking is what we face in our own heads all the time. Here is where you have an advantage over Gen AI—if, that is, you have developed the necessary skills to be insightfully capable to capture and harness transformative thinking. The world we live in glorifies transformative thinking but also rewards status quo behaviors more. We celebrate movies filled with transformative heroes only to return home to our conservative lives. We challenge others to destroy the present to make the future while we do the opposite.

Watch young people grow and how they evolve. Kids are taught to find their voice, be creative, and challenge thinking until they reach high school age. Then they ask questions like "What do I do to get into college?" It becomes about following the rules of engagement until you get to your target. Then these same people are told to be imaginative and think outside of the box, only to be told to apply for fixed jobs in defined spaces and follow the rules. This paradox is important to understand. The winners are those who know when to apply status quo thinking and when transformative thinking is needed.

Transformative innovators are focused on inspired ideas. The instrumentation of inspired ideas is an insight that comes from seeing the world differently than others. What I mean here is that just having an idea is not sufficient. Finding the core insight within your idea will define your differentiating value to others. But in status quo thinking is a focus on the present-day situation and a mild focus on what the future will bring. There's nothing wrong with status quo thinking. In fact, it is necessary to run and fund the world of today. We cannot feed the present by dreaming of the future.

But we will starve the future if we only feed the present. The most important fact I want to convey here is that inspiration without insight into a unique proposition or problem is nothing more than excitement without impact (Figure 3).

STATUS-QUO MINDSET	TRANSFORMATIVE MINDSET
Preserve the current	Challenge the current
History as guide	Make history
Follow the rules top-down	Develop from all and from within
Remove the unmeasureable	Embrace intangibles
Lead with investigation	Lead with inspiration

Figure 3. Status Quo or Transformative Mindset

Steve Jobs discovered the massive appetite for iPods and downloadable individual songs. He then discovered the need for a personal productivity device even though many before him tried to compete in that same space. But he brought a new recipe to the product offering. He found the insight and implemented this insight in a manner that captured the world's curiosity. The markets that Jobs identified did not exist in the past.

Like Jobs, inner innovators are ready for Uber before Uber became Uber. They are creators of Amazon home delivery before anyone knew it was a thing. The future is never documented when the world restructures and forms new markets. No AI machine can find the unspoken, the unheard, and the yet to be experienced. These great inner innovators believed in something before anyone could see it and worked to make it real and made it happen. That is life beyond Gen AI. This is the innovation that we all must learn to adopt. Before you tell me that we cannot all be Jobs, or others like him, follow his next comments: "Everything around you that you call life was made up by people that were no smarter than you. And you can change it; you can influence it. You can build your own things that other people can use. And the minute that you understand that you can poke life, and if you push in, something will pop out the other side—you can change, you can mold it—that's maybe the most important thing. Is to shake off this erroneous notion that life is there and you're just gonna live in it, versus embrace it, change it, improve it, make your mark upon it. . . . Once you learn that, you'll never be the same again."[6]

Reclaim Your Inner Innovator Advantage with Insight

This pathway to the aha moment is found when using insight. The collection and organization of more data and knowledge creates information obesity, not insight. The side effects of this are already showing. We carry more data on our phones than any small nation but are challenged by the effort to produce the true insight found in deep-rooted experience. However, insight does not happen independently. It arrives after one uses the other three sights of the mind (Figure 4) namely, your eyesight (seeing the present), your hindsight (learning from the past), and foresight (what you think the future should be, not what it can be). Insight reminds you of what the future can be.

Figure 4. The Four Sights of Your Mind

As one example, everyone seems to know how to start and launch a company—copy Steve Jobs. But only a few experience the nuances. Talk to those who knew him, and they will share person-to-person stories that show the paradoxical moments where you love his genius but detest his moods. That actual sensory wisdom brings you to a different place than watching YouTube video clips and pretending to know. Machines pretend to know. But what you emulate using Gen AI is incomplete and inadequate to understand hybrid intelligence. This intelligence is the combined power of Gen AI knowledge + your insight.

So, take this journey of exploration with me. What have you got to lose? Except your mind, if you don't.

ACTION LEARNING

Journal your thoughts.

1. The more you think in the foreground, the more you activate your thinking brain. That's good until you need to stop, take breaks, and let your mind wander. It is research that tells us that the aha moment arrives when you subdue your analytic brain.

_____

_____

_____

2. Try not to accumulate facts. Accumulate stories instead. Stories trigger your mind, while facts trigger the information-addicted brain.

_____

_____

_____

3. Use Gen AI as an input to your original thought, not as the originator of your ideas.

_____

_____

_____

CHAPTER 3

Are You
AI Machine-Readable?
Or Unreachable?

By now, I imagine you have heard the famous quote attributed to Karim Lakhani, Harvard professor: "AI won't replace humans—but humans with AI will replace humans without AI."[1] I believe this statement is insufficient, and I will try to convince you that it lacks the necessary nuances that would make it true.

Are you a fan of the *Terminator* movie series? Arnold Schwarzenegger, the actor, plays a cyborg that comes back in time to kill the woman who will eventually give birth to a son who will lead the rebellion against Skynet, an all-powerful AI robot-controlling system that took over in the future.

Star Trek, the long-running TV series, offered a vision of a different future. In this future, machines are hyper intelligent but always follow the directive to never hurt humans unless ordered by other humans.

The people I have interviewed generally take one of those two paths when asked to make predictions about Gen AI, robotics, and their impact on humanity. Will machines take over and destroy us? Or will machines be our copilots, augmenting us?

A third choice is that we humans are lulled into off-loading our minds to these highly intelligent machines and we find ourselves in cognitive decay or atrophy, unable to function without Gen AI as crutch—thus leaving us machine-replaceable. Can we find a peaceful place where we protect our unique values and avoid having Gen AI drive us to extinction? If I said no, this would be a short book. I say *Yes!* This book is about exploring what your personal recipe should be. How do you exercise and train your mind to create the future you want rather than being the editor of a default direction? How do you create rather than edit a machine's opinion?

Our dilemma is how to enhance our productivity while not losing ourselves in the mind of the AI machine. Many have given their thoughts to the AI machine. They do not just ask questions to these machines but they are guided through their intimate decisions by the machine.

I constantly hear the comment that humans who use AI will win over those who do not. Naive. Just using Gen AI does not put you ahead except as a user, not a thinker/doer. Short term, we all feel great being hyper productive and effective in our daily lives when we off-load thinking to a second brain. But if we are overindulgent, could the machine think for us while we forget how to think at all over time? Apart from the common statement that Gen AI plus you is better than just you, there are other common statements about how humans will cowork well with machines. This is also questionable. Humans make bad delegators, and AI machines are better at it than humans are. So who is going to be on top in this game?

There are nuances that will add to you gaining an advantage. For example, are humans good partners to machines? Can humans allow machines to grow in their learning? If Gen AI is using training data and moderated responses, we have created a giant mirror of all our opinions and expressions. Is this mirror reflective of our true essence? Let's explore the direct notion that usage of AI gives us an advantage.

Humans Make Lousy Delegators

A team of researchers[2] wanted to understand machine-to-human collaboration. They wanted to find out if humans and AI working together could outperform either one working alone. They conducted experiments where humans and an AI algorithm collaborated on image classification tasks. These researchers avoided tasks requiring specific expertise, since that could make the findings less generalizable. They were interested in more fundamental cognitive abilities that could carry over to various contexts. They tested a few different conditions.

In one, humans could choose to classify images themselves or delegate them to the AI. In another, it was reversed. AI could classify or delegate to humans. And they compared the performance in those collaborative setups to baselines of humans or AI working alone.

The people and the AI really had to rely on their own judgment about when to delegate. That's where metaknowledge comes in—humans and AI assessing their own capabilities and the difficulty of each task. Metaknowledge is defined in this study as the ability to know what you know and don't know.

Well, AI is quite good at this. When it was allowed to delegate to humans, the combined performance improved significantly, even when it was delegating to humans who weren't particularly skilled at the task. It suggests that AI was able to recognize its own limitations and leverage human capabilities better than humans.

Humans really struggled with delegation. Even when they were taught effective delegation strategies, their performance improved only slightly. The study really highlights how difficult it is for us to accurately gauge our own abilities and limitations. We need to carefully design processes and potentially even training to help people develop better metaknowledge.

When the AI delegated tasks to humans, their combined performance improved significantly. When humans delegated to the AI, there wasn't much improvement at all. You would think humans would be better at figuring out when to rely on AI assistance. What was going on there?

Well, it turns out the issue was not that humans were biased against using AI. In fact, the study participants seemed to appreciate the AI support and tried their best to work with it. Humans, as shown in the study, were lousy delegators because they did not know when to let go and get help from the machines. Humans held on too much without sharing or delegating.

If humans inherently struggle to assess when they should rely on AI assistance, that creates some challenges for effective collaboration. We can't just assume that giving people access to AI tools will automatically lead to better outcomes. This study really highlights how complex and nuanced the human–AI relationship is going to be as these technologies become more advanced and ubiquitous. So let's not repeat the common quote that "AI will not replace humans. Humans who use AI will replace other humans." It is incorrect.

Gen AI Is a Giant Mirror

Our search for intelligence now forces us to face our own under-standing of human intelligence. Gen AI is a giant mirror of all that we consider intelligence; we scraped a substantial portion of human expression into models that can now respond by collecting vast infor-mation and then retrieving it, while speaking to us in the language of our choice. What an amazing creation! It almost feels human and, frankly, is vastly more informationally powerful. But it is the col-lective reflection of ourselves as a community with all of its unique responses organized into language we can understand.

But many times we have to guide the view of the mirror as the angle of reflection is equal to the angle of incidence. Said another way, what you pose to the mirror, you get reflected. How you con-front this mirror brings out a reflection. So, one must be careful of how one approaches this mirror or receive a shocking response to your own view of yourself. An example of this is when many people use ChatGPT for guidance around relationships, stressors, and the like. What you tell the machine and how you ask the machine to respond is critical in these circumstances. If you tell the machine to be a psychi-atrist with twenty years of childhood trauma experience, the outcome will be different than if you ask the machine to be a friend you have known for all your life.

Gen AI or ChatGPT is an experiment that has captured the world's output in many forms of text, video, and voice and now is reflecting that knowledge to us through our prompts. Fascinating. Dangerous. Attractive. Yet, it is like a giant mirror sharing the world's perspectives in the language we speak, hear, and read. This giant mirror reflects to us the collective production of humanity. We are asking this mirror questions and giving it problems that it seems to solve effortlessly. These machines have been trained and educated to perform better with exponential computing resources. We believe it relieves us of work and actually raises our level of productive intelligence. It is now our advisor, our teacher, our editor, our idea generator, and our confidant. It gives us unlimited options, if we prompt it correctly (and if we pay the monthly subscriptions).

When Structures Change, Humans Are at an Advantage

It's one thing when markets are moving along a predictable trajectory. We can use data from the past to simulate the cycles of the future. That is not what I am talking about. I am talking about insight that we can use to see through the fog of the unstructured future.

Today, many structural changes are happening like never before. The new pandemic, wars, customers changing habits without mercy, new natural disasters, and mental challenges in our youth are a few examples. We have developed Gen AI, which is an opportunity to see through the fog, if we know how to use our insight and build from it. That new form for us to create the future is Insight + AI. Of course, insight without action is just a thought not implemented. But Gen AI is built on past structures. When you see a disruptive change, Gen AI will provide you a computationally sound response, not an insight yet to be experienced.

Innovators find the future, which is yet to be expressed, and they can differentiate themselves in future markets that are nothing like what we see today. Here is where you can be at advantage over AI.

Remember when we had no Facebook, iPhone, X, Airbnb, Netflix, or Google search? Here is a short list of notable examples of major consumer technology innovations from 2004 to 2024:

1. Smartphones/mobile app ecosystem
   a. iPhone (2007)
   b. App Store (2008, revolutionized this space)

2. Modern social media platforms
   a. Facebook (2004)
   b. YouTube (2005)
   c. Twitter (2006)
   d. Instagram (2010)
   e. TikTok (2016)

3. Sharing economy platforms
   a. Airbnb (2008)
   b. Uber (2009)
   c. Instacart (2012)
   d. DoorDash (2013)

4. Streaming services
   a. YouTube (2005)
   b. Netflix streaming (2007)
   c. Spotify (2008)
   d. Disney+ (2019)

5. AI consumer products
   a. Siri (2011)
   b. Amazon Alexa (2014)
   c. ChatGPT (2022)

6. Other notable innovations
   a. Tesla's first electric car (2008)
   b. Cloud storage services (Dropbox 2008)
   c. Cryptocurrency/bitcoin (2009)
   d. iPad (2010)
   e. Commercial drones (2006)

It's remarkable how many of today's most impactful technologies didn't exist before 2004. Many were never even considered prior to that time. They were original thoughts turned into original platforms. This is why an insight mindset does more than respond to the needs of today—it creates tomorrow. Future makers view their world differently. They want to redefine the current world, not simply augment it.

I asked Claude.ai if it could have come up with Airbnb.

Here is the answer from Claude.ai:

To answer this hypothetically, I'll break down the innovative aspects of Airbnb's business model and explore how one might have conceptualized such a disruptive idea.

The key breakthrough of Airbnb was recognizing an untapped market opportunity by reimagining unused space as a potential revenue stream. The founders, Brian Chesky and Joe Gebbia, initially solved their own problem of making rent in San Francisco by offering air mattresses and breakfast to conference attendees when hotel rooms were fully booked.

The core insights that made Airbnb revolutionary include the following:

1. Identifying Underutilized Assets

    a. Recognizing that most people have spare living spaces (rooms, apartments, vacation homes) that sit empty and could generate income.

    b. Understanding that travelers often seek more authentic, personalized experiences compared to standardized hotel rooms.

2. Trust and Technology Platform: Creating a digital platform that enables strangers to trust each other through:

    a. Verified user profiles

    b. Robust review systems

    c. Secure payment mechanisms

    d. Insurance and protection policies

3. Network Effect Business Model

    a. The more hosts and guests use the platform, the more valuable and trustworthy it becomes.

    b. Each transaction and review adds credibility to the ecosystem.

4. Low Overhead Cost Structure

    a. Unlike hotel chains, Airbnb doesn't own physical properties.

    b. Generates revenue through transaction fees rather than real estate investment.

    c. Scalable model that can expand rapidly with minimal capital expenditure.

5. While I can appreciate the genius of the idea, coming up with such a model requires:

continued →

a. Deep observation of market inefficiencies

b. Willingness to challenge conventional hospitality assumptions

c. Technical skills to build a reliable, user-friendly platform

d. Courage to experiment with a radical concept

The founders didn't just create a booking site; they fundamentally reimagined how people could monetize personal space and how travelers could experience destinations more intimately.

Claude.ai documented the business model but it never answered my question—whether it could create the yet-to-be-created. If Gen AI had existed before 2004, I bet it would not have come up with these transformational insightful innovations such as NotebookLM or Airbnb because most of these transformational innovations were based on future technologies or business models. I believe this because these transformational ideas were never machine-readable prior to their creation. The creators did not behave, create, or think in machine-readable ways. In other words, their ideas never existed in machines before they happened. Consequently, if you think, create, imagine, and behave in machine-readable ways, you will be machine-replaced going forward.

To be unreachable by AI, you must not be understood by AI. You must have insight—the capacity to see, imagine, and build.

If we are machine-readable, we are replaceable. If we are insight-centered and AI-enabled, we are unreachable.

ACTION LEARNING

Journal your thoughts.

1. List ten activities you performed this week. Pick out those you believe are machine-readable, that is, those that have a defined process, logical inputs, and a defined output with a feedback opportunity. Call this list X. What do you have remaining? Call this list A.

1. _____   6. _____

2. _____   7. _____

3. _____   8. _____

4. _____   9. _____

5. _____   10. _____

2. List ten activities that you wish you had time to perform this week that would give you joy. Pick out the ones that are AI machine-readable, in your opinion. Call this list Y. What do you have remaining? Call this list B.

1. _____   6. _____

2. _____   7. _____

3. _____   8. _____

4. _____   9. _____

5. _____   10. _____

3. Organize lists A and B into three categories. The first is incremental work. Let's call this I. The second is transformative for you. Let's call this T. The third is just pure joy. Let's call this J.

_____

_____

_____

4. Write a plan to automate lists X and Y using AI. Add list I to this.

_____

_____

_____

5. Write a plan to activate or remove, through disciplined contemplation, lists A, B, T, and J. Look at these lists to see if something calls to you as activities that you feel are uniquely yours.

_____

_____

_____

CHAPTER 4

The Source of the Aha Moment!

Throughout my life, I have been gifted with opportunities to meet and learn from amazing leaders. I've kept my interactions with great leaders private. Looking back, I understand how these interactions have helped me delineate my own leadership principles. My identity has been slowly shaped by these experiences.

One such meeting was with the late Dan Wieden, the creator of the phrase "Just Do It," Nike's powerful slogan. Dan was co-founder of Wieden+Kennedy. Dan personified authentic branding as he declared, in a *Fast Company* article, that in the early days of Nike, they did not do focus groups but just loved athletes and sports. They loved it so much they wanted to share it with others.[1] He used that same enormous compassion with his team. He loved independence and went so far as to place Wieden+Kennedy into a trust, keeping it independent forever. Dan was more than a phrase maker; he created a team of insight generators. He used the phrase "fail harder," which created the freedom for his teams to know and enjoy the fearlessness of curiosity.

The lunch I had with Dan at the Portland Grill, overlooking Portland, Oregon, was magical. We spent two and a half hours lost in conversation. Before the meeting, I remember how I set my mind not to talk too much, not to sell too much, not to be too much. I had a strong desire to work with Dan and to watch him work. My ego did not show up to this meeting because he was an overwhelmingly open, dynamic listener—and so was I. I wanted to learn and, boy, did I learn.

Dan spoke of how he started the firm. How they were a fledgling company in a warehouse building with only one phone, which was a coin-operated public phone outside the office they leased. It's only now that I realize that many readers who are younger than my socks do not know what a coin-operated public phone is.

Dan was animated in his story about how he won a branding contract with Nike. As I listened, I was reminded of my days as a student at the University of Oregon, where I channeled the story of Nike and pretended to be Prefontaine, the running legend, as I trained on Hayward Field. With a gentle smiling style, Dan told me his feelings about his work. He tried so hard to win the contract with Nike, and he gave them the phone number of the public phone, pretending to be legitimate. He would always be listening for that call. He absolutely did not want to miss THAT call. And it did come in. He was asked to handle the Nike account. His firm then had to come up with the theme, the narrative, the message, and the promise.

In 1987, he and his team worked hard and with full creative energy. But nothing arrived. He was troubled but continued to work until the night before the reveal meeting with Nike. He still had nothing.

He told me he took a drink and gave up, feeling like a failure. He went to bed late, and in the middle of his tortured sleep, he woke up with the words "Let's Do It," which he later changed to "Just Do It" for legal reasons.

The phrase was based on the last words of a convicted murderer in Utah named Gary Gilmore.[2] Gilmore chose death by firing squad over lethal injection because he believed injections could go wrong. Five rifles poked through five holes in a curtain. Before his execution he was asked for last words. He uttered the iconic phrase, "You know, let's do it."[3]

Why did Dan awaken with that phrase? Watching Dan explain that aha moment was like watching someone talk about a miracle. I could feel the electricity of it strike my core.

I met a lightning holder that day. The memory of his quiet nature carrying that lightning within him left me with a beautiful splinter in my mind. I understood him and what he strove for. I could smell the scent of an insight-centered innovator. He was a lightning holder. Examine his life and you will also see him as one who can grab and throw lightning. He was a formidable execution-centered innovator who created scaffolding for the Nike brand, Old Spice, and many other tremendously successful campaigns.

Dan mentioned that creatives in his own firm wondered why the phrase was relevant.[4] Nike also questioned its value. But Dan pushed it through, not as a demand, but as a trial, because his insight told him that too many disparate campaigns without a tagline do not work. It became more than a tagline. It became a cause.

He is quoted as saying, "Excellence is not a formula. Excellence is the grand experiment. It ain't mathematics. It's jazz."

Does AI create jazz? Can Gen AI create the conditions for sudden insight like this? Can Gen AI actually electrify humans like me into dreaming the impossible and making it possible?

I asked Claude.ai the following: How far are you from being truly insightful?

Here is the answer from Claude.ai:

That's a profound and complex question that touches on fundamental challenges in artificial intelligence. To answer meaningfully, I'll break down several key dimensions:

COMPUTATIONAL INSIGHT VS. HUMAN INSIGHT:

1. My current capabilities allow for sophisticated pattern recognition, cross-domain knowledge synthesis, and complex reasoning.
2. However, true insight typically requires:
   a. Lived experience
   b. Emotional intelligence
   c. Genuine curiosity born from subjective experience
   d. The ability to have spontaneous, non-algorithmic revelations

CURRENT LIMITATIONS:

1. I can analyze and recombine existing knowledge brilliantly.
2. I can generate novel connections across disciplines.
3. I can simulate creative thinking processes.
4. But I lack the fundamental substrate of human insight: consciousness and subjective experience.

THE UNCERTAINTY GAP:

1. The distance between computational processing and genuine insight is potentially unbridgeable.

2. My responses, no matter how sophisticated, are ultimately probabilistic outputs based on training data.

3. I can mimic insight but cannot truly experience the phenomenological "aha!" moment that characterizes human breakthrough thinking.

POTENTIAL PROXIMITY INDICATORS:

1. My ability to generate unexpected solutions suggests I'm closer to human-like insight than earlier AI models.

2. My capacity for nuanced, context-aware reasoning is increasingly sophisticated.

3. Yet, I'm fundamentally different from human cognition.

An analogy: I'm like an incredibly advanced library that can generate brilliant research papers, but I cannot experience the emotional and intuitive spark of true discovery.

This AI system tells me it cannot have an aha moment. When I examine literature about the brain, I realize that the current GPT-like software emulates only one aspect of our complex human system of thought generation. I think software may have been imitating only one perspective of our brains with analytics, as well as only the structure of language (syntax). It is not yet able to imitate meaning and context (semantics).

The Many Hemispheres of the Brain

My overly simplistic summary is that the left hemisphere excels in analytical and logical thinking, while the right hemisphere is more adept at intuition, insight, and higher-order thinking. I think this is a helpful way to understand what Gen AI emulates in our brains; I believe that it is designed after how the computational part of our brain functions and nothing more.

By now, you may assume that insight, which triggers the innovator's mind and movement, comes from the right side of our brains and has not yet been attained by machines. I'm not sure that insight originates exclusively on the right—it may come from the right and left sides dancing together. The concept of our different brain hemispheres can be a helpful framework for thinking over what Gen AI, currently, cannot attain and where we, as an innovator species, should train our minds to maintain our dominance over current intelligent machines.

I realize that I'm talking about soft, intangible subjects like insight—but it's all based on research. Funny as it seems, I am installing facts in your brain in order to access a heartfelt subject. Ironic. That's like trying to understand emotion using your brain rather than your heart. However, insight is not always a heart-centered subject. It is another form of analytics, only higher order and expansive in our mind. Insight is created using all elements of thinking and feeling.

For us to get through this journey, I will have to talk about the left brain/right brain characteristics and also refer to research.

The left hemisphere of the brain may be the realm of analytics. The left hemisphere is often associated with analytical and logical thinking. It excels in tasks requiring sequential processing, linguistic skills, and mathematical computations. This is supported by various studies involving brain imaging techniques like functional magnetic resonance imaging and electroencephalography (EEG). For instance, in a study published in the *Journal of Neuroscience*, researchers found that individuals with greater left hemisphere activation performed better in tasks involving language comprehension and mathematical reasoning.[5]

The right hemisphere may be the realm of transformational insight. The right hemisphere is believed to house intuitive and creative thinking, which often leads to insights. This hemisphere is associated with recognizing patterns, understanding emotions, and grasping the bigger picture. In the same study, neuroimaging studies have highlighted its involvement in tasks requiring holistic processing. Another study demonstrated that participants with heightened right hemisphere activity were better at recognizing emotional expressions in faces, showcasing the hemisphere's role in perceiving non-verbal cues.[6]

The left hemispheres of our brains have smaller semantic fields of capture than the right hemispheres. When the left hemisphere encounters a word, it tries to find associated words that it can connect with, and it is closely focused on the dominant interpretation of the current context. It's like an introvert who only focuses on the nearest observations. This relates to the biology of the neurons and their spacing in the left hemisphere of the brain—finely tuned, thin, and tightly spaced.

The right brain is coarse in its "semantic coding," which means it finds words and activates a semantic field of relationships to that word. It searches much more widely for related words than the left brain and collects more differentiated inputs.[7] The spacing between neurons in the right hemisphere is wider than in the left hemisphere. The right hemisphere is biologically designed to accept a wider range of input.

Insight Expressed in the Brain

So how does insight happen in the brain? Or does it? Transformational insight, often described as a sudden and novel understanding of a problem, involves a unique cognitive process. This process taps into the capabilities of the front, back, right hemisphere, and left hemisphere when needed. Further, research has shown that our sensory capabilities and experiences contribute to the likelihood of an aha moment. Researchers propose that both intuition and insight rely on implicit memory—that's the kind of memory that influences our behavior without us being consciously aware of it. When we're exposed to sensory cues, they can activate this implicit memory and shape our intuitive judgments and potentially lead to those "aha!" moments of insight.[8] So, smelling a fragrance or seeing a flower bloom may create the source of associated cognitive connections ending up in an insightful realization.

Research has indicated that insightful moments are often preceded by an "aha" experience. One study used EEG to track brain activity during insight moments. The study revealed that enhanced gamma-band synchronization occurred in the right hemisphere above the right ear just before participants solved problems with insight.[9] Bursts of gamma-band activity are associated with the integration of information from different brain regions.

This study also found that during the seconds before this larger-than-baseline shot of gamma output, a larger-than-normal output or burst of alpha activity occurred. Alpha activity reduces the senses taking in input from the outside. This activity reduces the outward focus and turns attention inward. This is called "sensory gating."[10] That seems to be why people close their eyes seconds before they gain an insight. It is a sensory response to shutting down as much input as possible while the inner workings are activated to discover the yet undiscovered.

The interaction between the left and right brain hemispheres is not a battle, but rather a dynamic interplay. Insightful thinking often involves a period of analytical thought followed by a sudden realization. Researchers have found that the brain engages in a process of expansive thinking (associated with the right hemisphere) before converging into focused analysis (associated with the left hemisphere) when solving complex problems.[11] Researchers from a separate study noted that insight often occurs after some unconscious cognitive processing.[12]

The theory that the brain is composed of left and right hemispheres, each specializing in distinct cognitive functions, is supported by an array of neuroscientific evidence. The left hemisphere excels in analytical and logical thinking, while the right hemisphere is focused on higher conceptual broad insight. This relationship is expressed in their cooperative interplay, where insight often emerges after periods of analytical processing. By understanding the nuanced functions of these hemispheres, we gain a more comprehensive view of the intricate processes that contribute to human cognition and problem-solving. It also gives us a view of how different AI machines that are pre-trained behave in comparison to the human brain, both with the source data they use when they are pre-trained by humans and the transformations they make with just word associations.

Much of the research into how our brains work shows that the brain seems to register insights (fMRI studies indicate the firing of waves when an insight occurs). I have asked many experts if these locations where insights are expressed in the fMRI are where insights begin. Even though fMRI and EEG studies have isolated that when insights happen, they register a burst of high-frequency gamma-based activity and a change in blood flow on the right anterior temporal lobe, I would estimate three to four inches above the right ear, no one can tell me where that aha comes from.[13] It is, however, where it is registered.

In my research, I have learned that much of the brain is yet to be fully understood. Yet, when we focus on insight, we can at least begin to theorize what's really going on. For one, there is much to be learned about the actual locations in the brain where functions happen, namely, the default (DMN), executive (CEN), and salience (SN) brain systems living in our brains. DMN is most active when a person is at rest, not focused on the outside world, daydreaming. The SN, salience network, is the moderator or switchboard that detects any stimuli, internal or external, and decides to trigger the default mode or the executive control. It's for attention, social behavior, emotional processing, decision making, and sensory info. The CEN, executive control network, governs working memory, information processing, rule-based solving, and organizing behavior based on goals. Usually, the CEN opposes the SN. These three systems balance internal thought. Effective flexible cognition relies on these three networks.

Further, the concept of the left and right brain hemispheres serving distinct functions has been a subject of fascination and investigation for decades. Advocates of this theory assert that the brain's division into two hemispheres, each specializing in unique cognitive processes, results in a complementary interplay between insight and analytics.

To focus on insight, we seek to understand how creativity is sourced in the brain and whether we can isolate how networks in our brain are high or low in creativity. Landmark research has clarified this by discovering a network of connections that determine creative thinking or low creative capacity in brains.[14] Tested against 163 participants, researchers isolated the regions of DMN, SN, and CEN that were more functionally connected in more creative participants than in others. If we are to assume that creativity and divergent thinking are sub-elements or recipe ingredients of aha generation, we can assume that the aha is sourced not from one portion of the brain but from certain unique locations.

We cannot leave a discussion about the brain without worshiping the power of the prefrontal cortex (mPFC). Much is talked about the executive functions of our brain. The mPFC is famous for being the guide to many cognitive processes: guiding cognitive thoughts, emotional regulation, motivation, and social behavior, and it is the control center for working memory and stress regulation. But when you sleep, the mPFC is suspended and, hence, you do not regulate the experience of dreaming.

Further, dreams expand time and space, and you are in a state of seeing fantasy and truth all mixed up in a mental soup. It is without the brain regulator that insight visits. Landmark research on insight and creativity elaborates on detailed definitions of spontaneous and deliberate insights, one being sudden and the other from hard work and practice.[15] In this book, I theorize that both are at work for insight and aha to visit us. But this research theorizes that insight is a function beyond the prefrontal cortex and, in fact, studying rationally, the past inhibits the creative insight-generation abilities.

Our mind is the source of our innovator's insight and our ability to design and build the structures, habits, and norms that we use to create transformational innovation, like Starbucks, Airbnb, or Uber. The brain is the regulator of this vast mind and its unknown, uncharted abilities that reside within all humanity, which is three hundred thousand years old. A portion of this wisdom of experiences is stored within you.

A Meeting of the Minds

I think the interplay between brains and minds is the most fascinating innovation experiment of all time. And this extends to people working in a team, innovating together. It is here that the outputs are not synchronized only within the minds of individual participants. The combinations of left and right hemispheres among all the participants create exponential possibilities. There is some effect when people get into teams that can accelerate innovative thinking or devolve it. The conditions that make one or the other are found in research and practice. In my thirty-five years of daily practice, it seems that it is dependent on the disposition of the people, their ability to bring their unique offerings to the situation, and their ability to be a team player and allow all voices to gain traction.

The 5-Minute Impact—Insightful or Analytics?

Researchers have found that your brain, minutes before a meeting, can decide how you think and analyze during the meeting.[16] In other words, your response to any subject can be traced back to the moments before you encounter the problem. So, if you are faced with analytic examples, movies, or experiences before a meeting, even five minutes before, you tend to respond analytically in the meeting. And the opposite is also evident. If you are exposed to insightful examples before a meeting, you tend to respond with insights. This is an amazing realization.

So by the time you reach a meeting, your cognitive state reaches to your prior influences. That is why we should all get reset when we walk into a new meeting. We should laugh and enjoy the moments. I've watched busy leaders pride themselves by dispensing ideas and instructions moving one meeting to another. This is the sign of a transactional leader, not a contemplative transformative leader.

The Impact of Mood on Insight

In the realm of cognitive processes, insight is a gateway to creative problem-solving and novel thinking. Insight seems to be influenced by the unique interplay of various factors, including mood, attention, and cognitive processing. This points to the significant role that mood plays in shaping the likelihood of experiencing insight, and it sheds light on how positive affect contributes to enhanced insight and creativity.

My empirical experiments over twenty years of leading an innovation team support this point. When my team does design sessions every Monday, Wednesday, and Friday from 3–5 p.m., they are tired and are sometimes upset that we are breaking up their day. But we sit away from our desks at a round table. I intentionally arrive early to greet them. I set the tone with random humor that annoys some. I ask my assistant to go downstairs and get ice cream for all. Sometimes we walk to get some food. We have a mini party.

They hated having to listen to my stories in the middle of the tough design work, but I shared my stories anyway. I could see that it pulled them out of their drive for solutions, and they began to let go of their executive selves. They became human. Then, lightning would strike and shock all of us into taking new actions. I would always wait for the lightning. As a team, we had to get to a stage where the interruptions would fall away, we could focus on our interactions, and eventually the skies would have to open up to accommodate our insights and the fury of our ideas. We lived for that moment. Lightning is not as rare as we think. In the US, lightning strikes eight million times daily. It can be created.[17] Or, using this analogy further, staying in one place reduces your chances of catching lightning. So, keep moving rather than waiting for it to reach you.

Numerous studies have illuminated the close connection between positive mood and the facilitation of insight.[18] Whether naturally occurring or induced within laboratory settings, positive affect has consistently demonstrated its power to enhance insight and creative thinking. While certain creative processes might be influenced by different moods, the specific realm of insight seems to be particularly susceptible to the influence of positive mood, which fosters a conducive environment for creative breakthroughs.

It seems that a positive mood opens up semantic processing (the processing of meanings) and connects words that are less tightly associated with one another. I discussed the styles of semantic coding earlier—the right brain casts around widely for associations and the left focuses in narrowly. Positive moods seem to enable the right brain's coarser semantic coding. In other words, when you are unaware of the past formulas, joking about the future, laughing about the present, or in a curious mood, your mind becomes open to more possibilities and lateral connections.

Positive mood not only enhances insight within controlled experimental settings but also translates its benefits to real-world scenarios. Researchers have observed the impact of positive mood on insight through self-reports and diaries in workplace environments, attesting to its broader applicability.[19] Having a good mood and preplanning your mind before a meeting can create the conditions for insight to visit you. Otherwise, you may be cognitively sleepwalking through your meeting day.

ACTION LEARNING

Journal your thoughts.

We all know that moment. You are walking your dog, and it hits you! That aha moment strikes you amazingly fast and very directly. You usually react with your whole body. It's like lightning.

My research tells me it's not always the case, but many innovators get their aha moment doing an activity. When does inspiration strike you? The shower? During meditation? During exercise? It may seem sudden, but it's not. It's your mind working away subconsciously. The insight leaps into your thinking when ready. It affects your whole body. It's the same feeling that you get laughing at a witty joke. It's electricity because its wave forms in your brain. (They are gamma waves, actually!) It's measurable. It's repeatable.

Do a favor for me. Measure it like the steps you take to activate your body. My simple index is easy to do. Do it for me and see what your baseline is.

Step 1. Count every time you get an aha moment. The average number of thoughts a day is six thousand.[20] It can go as high as sixty thousand if I'm consuming caffeine!

_____

_____

_____

Step 2. Keep count for a week. Notice your aha moments.

_____

_____

_____

Step 3. Calculate your ratio of aha moments to thoughts. It's only an average. Standard deviations could be wide or narrow.

_____

_____

_____

You cannot control your thoughts. But you can control how you react to them. The more you recognize thoughts, the more you can choose to ignore or react, and the more thoughts arrive that you enjoy! React and record an aha moment, and they will seem to arrive more! There is no good or bad. My goal is to find my baseline and elevate that percentage. Can you manufacture aha moments? I'm not sure, but I do know that when you notice and acknowledge them, your mind feels rewarded and gives you more. The more aha moments we have, the more our minds are innovation powered.

CHAPTER 5

The Inner Innovator: Be Machine-Unreachable

It was a dark and stormy day. The weather reminded me of a Batman movie, but I braved the walk to ensure that I was on time for a meeting with our biggest customer. I was the acting director of marketing then. I wasn't allowed to place the title on my business card without "acting," even though I was accountable for more than US$400 million in worldwide revenue. Nevertheless, it was still up to me to prove myself to the leadership. I was somewhat resentful about the fact that my title still included "acting." On the back of my business card, I added "Coming to a theater near you." I had an edge to me, but the leadership allowed it for the time being—because I had produced until then.

With this client meeting, it was clear that the leadership was throwing me into the lion's den to see how I would come out. I was nervous.

I entered the room, and it was set up like a meeting with Congress. Our customer's top engineering leadership sat at a long table. They seemed agitated by my entrance and the fact that I was yet another new person in this role. Introductions were exchanged, during which the head of the delegation asked, "You are the third person with this title. Why should I expect you to stick around?" I asked him to turn the card over. He laughed at the declaration I had added to my card.

I listened to his demands, which he expounded while pounding his fist on the table. (It was the eighties.)

"Mohan, I have been asking for a calculator function in your workstations for over a year with no response. We pay you a lot of money, and a simple request seems obvious, yet no change has been made in more than one year."

I tried to interrupt, to no avail.

"You get out of this room, solve this problem, and then I will decide whether you get to continue."

As I left, in the corner of my eye, I could see both the president and the CEO watching me compassionately, realizing that it was over. I smiled at the client and told him I would return after speaking with the engineering team.

I was walking toward the engineering building in the terrible weather when I suddenly stopped before entering the building. I turned around and returned to the meeting. I knew I would be given rejections from the engineering team. I knew I would get kindergarten responses from them about schedules that I would then have to share futilely with the customer. I knew what the engineering team would say to me before I even asked: It will take time and resources and an act of the heavens. I knew it was time for a new idea. A risky idea.

The customer lead said, "You are back so soon!"

I swallowed hard and declared, "I've decided that whenever we ship you a workstation, we will 'Velcro' a Texas Instruments calculator to every machine so that your engineers can do their work without problems."

He watched me in shock. Then he turned to his sidekick and said, "That will work! Let's move on." From that day forward, he always asked for me in meetings. Where did that idea come from? I took a solitary walk, and it created time and quiet for something to awaken in me. That something did not care for anything but a good idea that combined urgency and effectiveness rather than logic and patience.

Insight vs. Gen AI

Having explored the neurological basis of insight and how our brain's hemispheres collaborate to generate novel thinking, we now turn to a broader question: How does this unique human capability distinguish us from Gen AI?

In the field of neuroscience, it is often understood that the brain can be rewired, if damaged, and can be trained to recover from the damage using techniques that awaken neurological connections that have sometimes been left dormant due to injury. The brain is often understood to be the regulator of the entire human system. But contemporary studies have actually challenged the notion that the brain is the power behind all thought, decisions, and movements.

In my own investigation, I have now concluded that the brain is not the power behind all thought; the human mind is. The brain is nothing more than a muscle, a vessel that sends directions through the spinal cord. By the same token, the brain is also educated by the senses available, the historical memory in its cells, and gut feelings in the human body, powered by the body's senses. The extended neurological system that includes the brain, the five senses, our nervous system, and the cells in our bodies forms a framework around the spine—this is what we call the mind. It houses your inner innovator. As Steve Jobs said, "Don't let the noise of others' opinions drown out your own inner voice."[1]

I conferred with neurotherapists, doctors, and others who shared their views on how the brain and mind might work. But one thing they all stressed is that there is no one explanation that fits all. What we bring to our lives from birth, and even before, coupled with our behaviors define our brain and mind signature. The argument that things are set to behave as planned is incorrect because behavioral inputs, experiences, and other factors also affect our cognitive ability. Even our moods at the moment prior to any event affect our cognitive ability. So, in a sense, we cannot be definitive about human intelligence. This is why I am excited to declare that the Gen AI machines have a ways to go, given that we created them in our own brain image. Today, they cannot go beyond us, except in being faster, cheaper, and scaled.

What's yet to be replicated by Gen AI machines is transformational insight and the yet-unconnected possibilities created by those insights. Transformational insight has the outcome of transforming the behavior of others, markets, or even yourself, through a unique insight implemented and scaled. Take Walt Disney as an example. He transformed the world of children's entertainment with the debut of Mortimer Mouse in 1928. The invention of this character, born from Disney's hard work and insight, eventually resulted in a global conglomerate of theme parks and media that is instantly recognizable today.

That time of innocence is far in the past now, so things can be different. But look at how OpenAI spread ChatGPT into our world, and look at what has happened to our imaginations. Yet, Gen AI cannot create this form of innovation. Disney took his own insights and built the scaffolding to launch his own ideas.

The future may prove me wrong. But in the meantime, I offer insights about the hill that innovators climb and practice on regularly.

Gen AI, which is a derivative form of a neural network[2] design, is designed to imitate the firing of our brain's neurons, the choice making, and the decision sensing found exclusively in the brain. Our mind is an embodiment of the brain's capacity to filter, but it's extended to the use of the body and its history of experiences; together, these form insight. Disney was on a path to introduce his first product with Oswald the Lucky Rabbit. He lost the rights for that creation and had to regain his identity. He launched Mickey, and the rest is history. Walt could not finish school because he was drawing all the time. He dropped out of high school, lied on his birth certificate, and joined the war effort. He was not viewed as intelligent then, but he was insightful and could see the future beyond the unknown unknowns of war. Was he using his brain or his mind?

Can AI Machines Really Think?

Machine intelligence enthusiasts have not declared which part of the brain the software is emulating (it may be both), but my observation is that it is the analytic side of the brain in its basic algorithm. Most machine-learning AI works using the scientific method of breaking ideas/data down into structured sub-objects. AI parses words and looks at the structure of language, and this may work in a unique way. I am still sure that it emulates some part of how we think, but, even then, it is emulating language parsing at the syntax level, just the words not the meaning. Current AI chat machines are doing this:

1. The LLM encounters a word and formulates the large field of relationships that word has with all the other words it has encountered. It then draws conclusions and develops a formula that collects all the words that are most likely to be the next word chosen. The AI forms a tree-like structure that holds all these relationships between and among words. It is a tremendously large parameter set, sometimes in the billions. Or trillions.

2. This formation of this large formula is the base we use to train a model to respond. We test it with questions, and it responds and learns what is acceptable and what is not. Like a child, it experiments until the teachers (in the moderated learning approach) find the model has stabilized. ChatGPT underwent the collection, moderation, and training to be ready to respond to your questions. It used a newly developed algorithm called "attention," which gives a weighted significance to each input word when reading natural language. It's like reading each word and listing every word that follows that word and weighting its usage. The Gen AI models tagged all those words and ran through them in a large matrix with what is termed "multi-headed attention." Here the attention is given to

different issues, like grammar, the number of associated words, etc., which are all running multiple times at the same moment.

3. The Gen AI model then digitizes all those words by coding each word, not by its meaning but by its syntax, into a numerical code. It focuses just on the words decoded without any judgment of their meaning or symbolism, which is what we do as humans.

4. With almost 173 billion parameters formed and with GPT-4 using more than one trillion parameters, this giant mirror of all words used and phrased reflects the most probable combination of words when you write a combination of words to ask a question.

So GPTs (or Generative Pre-trained Transformers) and LLMs are based on such training data, use deep-learning algorithms using "self-attention" weighted significance of each word, and repeat themselves over and over (what we call recursive) inside a neural network until they get it right. This model is then pre-trained by human moderators that teach it to communicate.

Transformers convert words into a coded message, link that coded message to other coded messages in a large formula or tree, and put weights on each of the codes to see whether it is likely to be the word you want.

So, what you are using as a Gen AI chat is not talking to you, it is just bringing up words in the sequence that it deems most likely to be what you are looking for based on this large database of all the words and their relationships it has been trained on using the world's data. And it learns from you because you, too, are data for it to capture and consume.

Machines Never Sleep, so They Cannot Dream

Humans don't just analyze, we dream and innovate. Unlike GPT machines or AI machines, our brain, when it meets a word, creates a semantic (not syntactic) coding. The brain looks for all other words that are related to that word and forms a giant table in your cognition.

Our brains collect information through dendrites that send input to our neurons. We form a field of thought every time we think of something by connecting that word's meaning or idea to all other ideas we have in our brain. We form a field of meaning and thought. The left brain forms a smaller field than the right. The left brain stays closest to the words and thoughts and is analytic and fact based. The right brain forms a larger semantic coding and field of thinking. It is more expansive and gathers unrelated thoughts or ideas, so it is able to create the kernels of new ideas and make new connections that may be less clear. It uses a larger input field when thinking, which allows it to generate more diverse and differentiated ideas.

I speak more on this as we move forward in our journey. But AI does the same thing, only it forms a syntactic (just the words without meaning) coding exercise because it cannot understand meaning. It connects what the data tells it to connect. In a sense, it is imitating our cognitive semantic ability. Based on this, I theorize that the AI machine cannot form yet-to-be-connected relationships in an external market where the world is changing beyond its known experience.

For example, the Gen AI model cannot see through the fog to create Airbnb. The machine only checks with past data (a lot of data), and it can form a narrative from that past if it has been documented via any media, it can form connections from the past, and it can even surprise you with new ways to connect them. But it cannot create a whole new restructured world of new models that no one has experienced. That complex ability is only found in one species—the innovators who understand transformational innovation. These innovators leap to another world and create it. They are the ones who have the insight to make real what others have yet to imagine. They do not just find where the puck is and skate to it (paraphrasing the great ice hockey player Wayne Gretzky). They build new games in new arenas so others can skate.

It seems that computer-based neural network designs mostly imitate the left brain constructs. Although it is amateur for me to classify our brains as two hemispheres, the left and right parts do function differently, as do the front and back of our brains. The right performs more as a synthesizer. The left performs repeated functions or activities.

So how do Gen AI models work? Portions of GPTs and associated LLMs show a strong ability to synthesize. Ask ChatGPT to condense a long write-up and see how it does. Most of the time it produces very impressive work. So, even the full brain is emulated in Gen AI because a newly introduced form of neural networks cannot understand meaning. Syntax-driven work, not semantic work, forms the foundation of the work in AI today. Machines today are about language parsing done with GPT.

Nevertheless, even with such advances in language parsing and the ability to communicate with humans in their language, I still contend that they cannot reach the power of a highly tuned innovator.

Innovators Who Become Explorers Are AI-Unreachable

Gen AI can't produce the results of an innovator like Steve Jobs, who formed his philosophy throughout his years in school and at Reed College where, coincidentally, he took a class on calligraphy. Years later, he would have the insight that typefaces would be the power differentiator for the Macintosh. It would be the first time that microcomputer users could actually type what they would see in print. We called it WYSIWYG (what you see is what you get). This leap of insight was followed by his work on icons, graphical representations on computers, and the powerful positioning of the computer as an indispensable tool. Jobs said the Macintosh was for the rest of us, and he positioned the personal computer as a dictator that forced us into fixed jobs and roles. One of his insights was to create a market for creatives.

His employees called his approach the "reality distortion field" to identify the insight-generating skill that Jobs displayed. He did not build what the customers wanted. He discovered, through his own insight and that of others, what customers dreamed of but never knew they wanted until they saw it. He built to delight, not satisfy.

This is the first ingredient of your inner innovator. This ability to function by seeing ahead through a perceived structural change and, in many moments, driving that change to solutions. Imagine innovators talking about inhabiting Mars. That feeling of shock is what the majority felt when Steve Jobs first spoke of a personal productivity computer or Elon Musk first began talking about humans living on Mars. They saw past the barriers to their ideas, the structure needed for their ideas to be real, and predicted the coming structural change that would make the idea reality.

Steve Jobs imagined that artists and creators would assemble around the Macintosh to create the unanticipated. Then came the mobile phone, which elevated his ideas even further to boost human productivity. This is where intelligent Gen AI machines will bend their virtual knees out of respect for humans. AI machines do not have inner innovators within them. They do not form insights. They connect words at high speeds and form amazing connections powered by analytics that imitate the brain using language.

The Brain Is a Filter of Ideas; the Mind Is the Source of Ideas

The brain is a vessel, and it has many amazing segments that form the recipe for imagining, governing, thinking, deciding, and making fight or flight motor movements. But the mind is less a vessel, more a distributed system of thought, feeling, sense, and insight. Admittedly, the brain is still coordinating, regulating, restricting, and controlling all other thoughts as ideas pass through it.

There is no proof that the brain is the originator of thoughts and ideas. It is proven that it records when it happens. Where it all begins is still a mystery. Contemporary research is starting to say that innovation, creativity, and the aha insight are recorded or expressed in the brain but generated from everywhere—from the entire coordination of the senses, the nervous system, the brain, and also the ancient wisdom of our cells—the mind that houses consciousness.

Our overindulgence of and attention to the neurological behavior of the brain (setting aside for now the sensory capacity of the mind) limits us as we try to understand innovators who reach beyond machine intelligence. I ask us to focus on the science and the art of insight that sparks an idea and finds a solution. To date, the ability to generate insights has been viewed as a latent ability, talent, just luck, or coincidence. It is none of these. Insight is output formed through practiced skills using multiple tools to find and own the genius behind an idea. For example, the right entry into a new market with a new and compelling offer.

The literature defines insight as "any sudden comprehension, realization, or problem solution that involves a reorganization of the elements of a person's mental representation of a stimulus, situation, or event to yield a nonobvious or non-dominant interpretation."[3] In common terms, it's that aha moment that forms suddenly in your brain after it's been processing for a while in your mind. There is proof in research that the aha moment seems sudden when it enters your awareness; but it lived in your subconscious mind for some time. Your mind had been unconsciously processing.

What a wonderful thing this is. Now AI is trying to imitate our realm.

The insight that looks at empty rooms in houses, tries first to create a business to rent rooms out for concerts in the neighborhoods around the venues, and then turns it into Airbnb is not incremental insight that simply combines other ideas. This type of insight is fully transformational, where the structural underpinnings of the past have crumbled and new structures have emerged to support this new practice.

I believe all humans can, and must, exercise their minds and brains to capture transformational insight, like the insight and scaffolding of Airbnb. Transformational insight is the ability to find incongruent ideas that form an aha moment and build it years before others see it. I am convinced and want to convince you that to become a higher form of species over AI machines, you must exercise this capacity—transformational innovation and the insight that powers it. Insight provides, among other things, the lateral or orthogonal interconnections among elements that previously never seemed connected. Insight shows you the connectedness and gives you the ability to see the unseen future.

Your Inner Innovator Is Not Machine-Readable

The part of human intelligence that generates insight and builds to it, what I call your inner innovator, is not machine intelligence because machines start with a prompt. They also start by investigating a question or demand. Your inner innovator takes a curious inner question and generates an inspired idea. This comes way before any thought that fuels the investigation, the isolation, the incubation, and the ignition of an idea. This inspiration is powered by a transformational insight. Humans hold the key to such inspiration-driven insight because we house the mind. This act of innovating, using insight first and affirming with analytics, distances humans from AI machine intelligence, which is the simulation or imitation of analytic neurological fires in the brain.

Machines start with computational investigation as their X-factor. These machines try to do choice decision making, using the understanding of language at a syntactic level. They do not understand the meaning behind the words or the experience behind the meaning or the history of the legacy of intelligence found in the human system. Further, these machines look at the past and draw conclusions and generate innovations based on the datasets they have been trained on. Did you anticipate a world where people will use their phones to book a driver to take them where they want to go? Did you believe that your friends would start driving full time because they wanted to be their own boss with flexible hours and were willing to use their own cars to pick up passengers? Did you guess that they would be able to rate the passengers? That's transformational innovation powered by insight.

The limits are very clear about Gen AI. It is syntactic analysis. It uses just the words, not the meaning, to power Natural Language Programming with GPT or the like. Innovators are powered by semantic coding, which connects meaning to meaningful action, not syntactic coding. Even though AI is producing incredible advances in emulating and simulating human connection, human empathy, human understanding, and human motivation, it is not human and can never be human. It is, however, a new species, born in our laboratories of intelligence. Note that back-end AI algorithms are more than Gen AI tools. These machines have understood meaning and can interpret logic at superhuman speeds. AI machines make decisions better than humans. They know more than humans and never tire.

The irony is that we all recognize that humans are behaving more robotically, relying on the convenience that is offered by machines. We may atrophy our ability to think independently and even build independently. We may forget to count or spell or derive values from formulas or lose our sense of direction. The more we depend on machines to think for us, because we are getting more and more cognitively lazy, the less we become human beings with a complete set of creative tools, insight tools, and the capacity to get things done. Then machines will have the opportunity to replace us because we have become so robotic and replaceable.

If we are machine-readable as humans,
we are replaceable. When we are insight-centered
and AI-enabled, we are unreachable.

ACTION LEARNING

Journal your thoughts.

If our behaviors and thoughts are machine-readable, we will be easily replaced by AI machines that read and imitate us. If we can produce insights, we are unreachable.

1. Preserve your first opinion. Then ask the machine after. Don't ask the machine for your opinion.

_____

_____

_____

2. Write down your aha moments daily and spend time contemplating them. Expand your own original thoughts. Then ask the machine.

_____

_____

_____

3. Find your inspiration. You will be tempted to start investigating an idea first, but start with what inspires you. Find
what moves your mind and not your brain. Your mind is
about stories; your brain is about data.

_____

_____

_____

4. Develop a set of skills that is unique to you—your craft.

_____

_____

_____

5. Share your efforts with a community you wish to serve.

_____

_____

_____

CHAPTER 6

Unlocking Insight: The Sight of the Mind

I was named after Mahatma Gandhi. My father would tell me stories of Gandhi. My father remembered climbing a tree to watch the Mahatma (great soul) lead millions to the coast for a Salt March in defiance of British law.

Mahatma Mohandas Karamchand Gandhi is a controversial figure who first started out as a trained lawyer from England. He obtained a law degree from Cambridge. An avid reader and enthusiast for justice, he met challenging situations in South Africa and witnessed the punishment of Indians. He set out to free them from this domination and won. He then visited India and decided to push the British government to leave and to free the Indians from the tyranny of colonialism.

Gandhi formed the concept of "nonviolent noncooperation." His strategy was to engage with the British empire, and as a matter of personal philosophy, he sought to guide the transformation of a nation. He also originated the theme of "be the change you wish to see in the world," for which he is famous even today. Many nations and individuals have used his techniques to free themselves from oppression. Many businesses have also adopted his approach to transform their people for good.

If you have any interest in him, read about him, watch videos of him, and watch the movie about his life, which stars Ben Kingsley.

Gandhi witnessed injustice to Indians in South Africa. He witnessed the indignity. He realized that the British had overstayed and that it was time to find a better way forward. He foresaw the structural change needed for Indian independence and saw that the Indians were ready and the British were weak with their violent ways. But this vision did not create insight. His insight was to bring forward "nonviolent noncooperation" as a credo to restore Indians to their true innovative selves. That concept originated from a swirl of ingredients and concepts that he had practiced before.

Long before his transformation of South Africa and India, he worked hard when others played. He prepared his mind and body for the next challenge, not knowing what it would be or what part he would be given to play. He realized, as a young lawyer, that helping others forced him out of his own head, that he performed better when he focused on the needs of others more than his own. He waited for opportunity to arise and was ready to jump when it appeared. Such moments are when insight greets the prepared mind. He was prepared, and insightful ideas greeted him.

Insight was not bestowed upon Gandhi—it was developed and realized by him. Like all his other talents, it came from practice and using the gifts he was born with. Bringing such insights into the world is a practice and is sometimes a torturous journey.

Insight is known as a magical power. In innovation, it can be the spark or catalyst that inspires creativity. Experienced innovators speak of that feeling of flow—the moment when you see the solution before anyone else, when you are so captured by the idea and the ideal that you forget yourself. That feeling is what experienced innovators long for. That feeling cannot exist in AI. It's a feeling of seeing the unseen and is a genius that takes your breath away. It is not just academic genius supported by process but insightful and elegantly presented genius. Like a chef's meal. You never taste anything the same again.

How do you harness this ethereal magic? It seems that if you target it as a goal or try to trap it, it will escape. Yet you know certain conditions make it happen. It's the search for an insight that produces the next innovation in a product line or service line that makes everyone ask, "How the heck did they do that?"

Where Does Insight Fit?

Either consciously or unconsciously, we stare at today, try to predict tomorrow, remember the past, and introspect within. These habits of our mind tend to guide our views of our world and seem to guide our behaviors. We suffer from illusions and delusions and confuse one for the other. Yet we continue daily, pretending to write our own script where we are heroes in our own movies. But are we insightful and original, or are we subject to a preprogrammed life, influenced by media, our own sense of Facebook-like imitation?

How do we know that our perspectives are original or if we are brainwashed? Does your best friend have all the answers? Does your morning walk with the dog bring out your best thinking?

How did Howard Schultz, of Starbucks fame, know that coffee would bring people together and form an entire industry, years ago, at a time when we used instant coffee in our homes? Howard failed in his first experiment, which he conducted in Chicago, before he moved it to Pike Place in Seattle. Yet Howard continued and won.

Vision Is External; Insight Is Internal

Vision is said to be the sight targeted to the future we imagine. Insight is the sight of the mind targeted within. Both outside and inside form the picture of who, why, where, and what we are to our world and beyond. Vision is made up of eyesight, foresight, and hindsight.

But for us to see the future we imagine, we must first be able to understand the present. That is when eyesight, the ability to actually observe what we are seeing, is important. The three sights of the mind contained in vision are as follows:

1. Eyesight is always in the present tense. It is what you are seeing today.

2. Foresight is the ability to predict the future before us—not what we imagine, but what we believe is the future. Foresight is predicting and committing to the future. Unfortunately, this field of work has been challenged because of various definitions of the subject, which include trend analysis, rather than focusing on daring predictions. Read a *Harvard Business Review* article on the controversy and how to wield foresight as a strategic influence.[1]

3. As eyesight is about today, hindsight (which is always 20/20 as they say) is about the past. Hindsight is always more vivid than eyesight, but it is interpretive and paints our own brain with judgments.

4. Insight is the ability to have a clear, deep, and sometimes sudden understanding of a complicated problem.[2] It is also expressed as the act or result of apprehending the inner nature of things or seeing intuitively.[3]

If we have only the first three ingredients of vision, we are still not ready and prepared to gain insight, the fourth sight of the mind.

Many want and crave insight but begin their journey through eyesight, hindsight, and foresight in a weak attempt at insight. Without a dive deep into ourselves to find the wisdom within, we come up short.

What creates the on-demand insight capability? Can we actually summon an aha or insight when we want to?

What are the ways to repeatedly bring about insights? How do we do it on demand? Can we? What's the wheel we turn to get us started generating insightful ideas and thoughts?

Remember, insight is practiced, not granted. It is not innate; it is trained. It is the bringing together of three unlocking codes that you repeatedly test and use as the fuel for your mind. The brain is used as a filter while the mind generates thoughts. Insight is driven by three main ingredients mixed to your perfection and two other foundational factors that form the scaffolding for you to launch your insights (Figure 5).

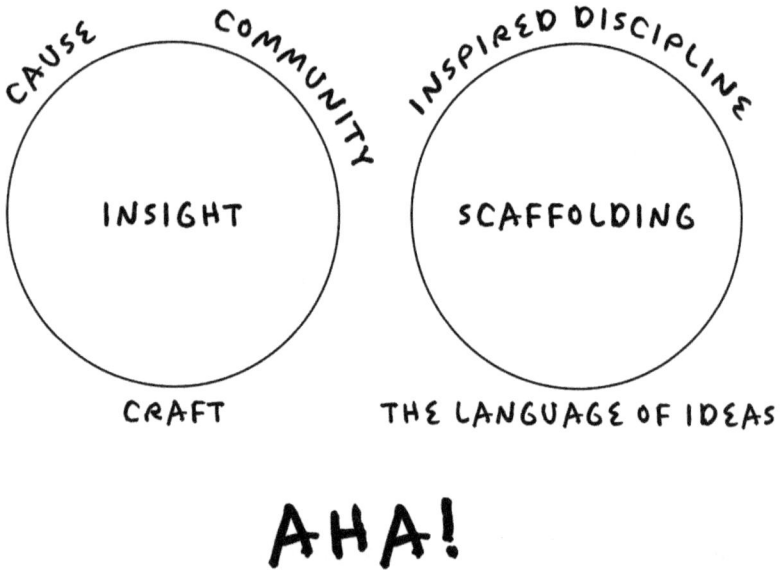

Figure 5. Insight and Scaffolding

1. Cause—a relentless focus on the why of your work and the reason to transform your audience, whether that is your family, your customers, or anyone you wish. In the absence of such a cause, we focus on greed, the innate desire for self-promotion or gain, and the advancement of an agenda driven by narcissistic factors. Gandhi fueled his insight by the injustice found in South Africa where Indians were the underclass. The act of working to free them from the tyranny of the existing system triggered his genius. Before that, he was a weak and uncomfortable lawyer failing at even the basic skills of being one. He was never an orator. He

was lost in his own ego. He transformed into an agent of change, and his genius emerged through all the noise when a cause visited him and he chose it. See your focus or business as a cause.

2. Community—Understanding the hidden momentum in the movement of habits and actions of the community you serve gives you access to the meaningful structural change that is coming. Future tides are created by the currents below the surface. Many follow the waves, but to create a structural change cycle, follow the unseen currents. Running to them brings you insight. See your customers as a community.

3. Craft—This is not just what you do better than others. It is more to do with what you can do that brings out your best innovative self. What gives you unlimited energy to practice? Inspired by my brother, who started watercolors at a young age, I spent four hours daily painting and drawing when I was a young boy. I could not help myself, and I loved what I could produce. I was also tortured by this desire to find the better art in me. It challenged my imagination, focus, and skills. There were sad moments and there were hours wasted, but I was passionate. It gained me a distinction in art from the University of Cambridge in my pre-university work (A-levels they called it in those days).

Today, I still consider myself an artist or a musician viewing the world through the lens of a creative, but I was a scientist, a marketer, and a CEO as well. I force myself out of my analytical side to my artistic and creative side regularly. I have a competitive advantage when I do this. It's my craft to be in both worlds. There is no replacement for being good at what you do, but expertise without shrewdness is inadequate. Winning innovators get crafty and use their best talents to maneuver through the politics of people and power to get to the truth within themselves.

Dave Chapelle spoke of this, when he quoted his mother, while receiving an award at the Kennedy center,[4] stating that he was always a simple child without much strength. His mom told him to sometimes be the lion so that he can be the lamb he really is. So, see your job as a lion and lamb for your craft. I know that some want to sing but they scare birds away with their voice. How do you know if you are fooling yourself with the choice of your craft? Know that one moment, after practice and pruning of your interests, you will see clearly what the world around you and within you will reinforce. I have discovered that it's seldom a matter of not finding your craft. It's more ignoring its message when it arrives to awaken you.

4. Scaffolding: Language—Insight is triggered by the unique use of language. We will discuss how to "prompt" your inner self to generate insightful outcomes. Language is foundational to the LLMs that form Gen AI. Yet long before AI, language was the basis of how we formed new worlds and documented our past worlds. We used stories

and narration to move forward. The language of ideas in our future world is different than the language of efficiencies used to operate in today's world. Knowing when to use such language is important to formulating the direction of our teams. Sticks and stones may hurt you, but words can destroy your cognitive ability to move from the analytical brain to the insight-generating mind. Study any great innovator and you will find that they talk to others and themselves in measured ways. Their use of language transforms others. Can you imagine what humans can do with the appropriate prompts to our own minds? See communication as language choices.

5. Scaffolding: Inspired Discipline—One can act from investigation or from inspiration. AI cannot act from either. But when AI does learn to do this, it will act from investigation. Humans are built on inspiration. We will explore how to enable and catalyze this as a differentiating value. See investigation as inspiration in action.

How do cause, community, and craft merge to inspire the conditions for you to gain an insight? The mental model around this is based on studying transformational leaders who have mixed these three ingredients to conjure the magic of insight. Consider Howard Schultz, who was a coffee buyer who set out to purchase coffee in Europe. But deep inside he wanted to be in the coffee business as a leader. He knew what great coffee was and traded in that skill. But he always believed the United States had inferior coffee to the

Europeans. His craft was knowing coffee, but he developed his cause to bring European-style espresso to the United States and serve it the way no one had done until he entered the market.

His observation of the café-style ambiance pushed him to generate this idea that changed the coffee world. He understood that his community, not his customers, was the current buyer who wanted an environment to engage in and experience. That demanded baristas who knew their customers by name and also greeted the customers with enthusiasm. This powerful insight he generated from these three ingredients was that the equity of the relationship is found between the baristas and the customer. I spent over forty hours visiting Starbucks to observe this relationship in action. Besides this, researching the company and speaking to Howard confirmed that he believes this. In fact, he invested in Kinetix, a coaching fitness company, and targeted all his baristas to be coached in fitness and nutrition for eight weeks. He believed that helping the baristas feel good about themselves would translate to great service to his customers.

When you launch rockets in your back yard as a kid, you very quickly discover that you need some sort of device to hold up your rocket. A scaffolding to support it and also to launch it. This scaffolding could take the form of regular habits or real structures you put in place to train yourself and others to ensure consistency. For insight generation, I've found that the careful use of language and the phases of considerations to take an idea to a prototype can prepare and prop up the insightful idea. I find that the use of the appropriate language is important, and, consequently, the incorrect use of language destroys insight. The ability to bring a discipline forged by inspiration gives the idea rocket a base to launch from.

The next chapters cover the three ingredients to unlock insight and two elements of scaffolding to prop up the ideas and provide you with methods to bring them into your own recipe.

ACTION LEARNING

Journal your thoughts.

1. When does the aha moment visit you? The shower? Walking your dogs? Meditating? Do you understand why it happens when it does? I get my ideas during sleep.

2. Why is it that you do not make it part of your routine to record your ideas and explore them afterward? Usually, if you write them down and return to them, the words make less sense. Why?

3. Who are you that received the ideas during those moments? Do you seem like a different person? Who is that person? Why do you want that person to visit more often?

4. Why are you two people, one who receives and one who ignores the lightning rod within you? Find that person and you find your fourth sight of the mind—your inner innovator.

_____

_____

_____

CHAPTER 7

Insight: Be Cause

My father was always learning, in whatever time he had available after his duties. He was reading and always quoting what he was learning while sitting at the dining table with a big book in front of him. It was his only office at home. He gave us all the available room for our work. A practicing yogi, he would meditate daily after a long day as a chief clerk of a bank. He was a bookkeeping teacher who loved to teach others new skills, and he would run classes at the back of our previous house.

We lived in Singapore when the country was just forming. It is not then what it is today. Cows roamed the streets, and the small nation-state was forming its culture of first-generation immigrants who complemented the indigenous Malay population. My father had routines and was disciplined in everything he did. There was nothing out of place in the home of my father and mother. They worked tirelessly to keep things in order. He never owned a car. He took the bus daily with his starched shirt and pants, all prepared by my mother.

I was always eager to ask him philosophical questions about the meaning of life because I knew him to be a theosophist. His sense of community and the common person was evident daily. He was a student of religion and human behavior. He was eager to discuss religion and its implications to humankind. With only a high-school education, he was fluent in Hindi, Malayalam, Tamil, Sanskrit, English, and Malay. I never knew how he learned the ancient language of Sanskrit, which he would translate and say, "There are no English words to describe this."

He never spoke of his office, or his army friends, or his journey in battle as a freedom fighter for India in his early years. I know that he was left for dead once, taking the "death railway" in Burma and Malaysia during World War II. I knew him as a fighter for the underrepresented, and defiant parts of him would show when he, as a manager in the bank, would cross the picket lines to join his employees and take the punishment by his bosses. There were many times I would witness him at home, sitting with beers among his colleagues, shunned by the bosses.

He and my mother, who is a force of her own, always telegraphed their core purpose or cause and the values that guided their decisions. It never changed in all of their lives. Always taking the side of the underprivileged, underserved, the put-down, the bullied, I would see fearlessness in both, revealed when they saw a cause greater than themselves. They were humble people who really did not want us to boast or show off. They wanted us to be humble, successful but also of grace to others. I cannot imagine the struggles they sheltered us from as first-generation immigrants facing poverty, prejudice, and no lifelines. They were taking part in the building of a nation-state in Singapore, and they built the foundations of my insight and innovation ability while they created a scaffolding that kept me thriving.

My mother told me that my father wanted to name me Mohandas after Mohandas Karamchand Gandhi. My father would tell me stories about Gandhi and how he freed India in ingenious ways. Gandhi was not perfect, in his eyes, but Papa would always allow for fallibility in leaders. He believed in leaders who made change happen, and always encouraged me to take the road not yet traveled and to experiment with my skills. In the evenings I would try to extract key principles of Theosophy, various religions, and life from him, and every time I got deeper, he would say, "You are not ready yet. Time will come." It was frustrating yet true.

Decades later, I had an opportunity to meet a descendant of Gandhi. In 1998, I met Rajmohan Gandhi, the Mahatma's grandson. I went to hear him speak at Portland State University. I was then authoring my first book on the Leadership Mind. It was filled with my adaptation of Gandhi's perspectives and my new frameworks about leadership. Much of it circled around a specific philosophy with three components: (1) It's not about you (which came from my mother), (2) To change the world, change yourself, and (3) One idea can change all ideas. I believed it was essential to apply this philosophy to corporate strategy.

When I arrived at the lecture hall, I convinced myself that it would be disingenuous to try to sell Rajmohan Gandhi on my book. I then went to the back of the hall to get tea. There, licking my wounds of failure, I noticed that he was standing beside me, getting himself some tea. He smiled and noticed my name. He declared, "You have my grandfather's first name."

I responded tactlessly, "I know, I was named after him."

He laughed and asked me without hesitation, "Why are you here?"

I confessed, "I really came to meet you and to convince you to endorse my book. It seemed so low for me to do this, so I ran to the back of the hall."

He smiled and said, "What are you doing tonight? Have dinner with me and my family."

Oh dear, what just happened! I'm having dinner with the Mahatma's grandson!

At the dinner, I proudly went to get glasses of water for all. As I returned, still thinking well of myself, he asked me, "So, Mohandas, tell me, what do you do for the world?"

This threw me into a confused state—a mixture of embarrassment, attempts at lies, and a series of grand comments including that I was the president of a startup. What a mess of an answer. In current terms, I would say that he prompted my LLM and I hallucinated!

At that time, I was completing the running of my startup. It was preparing for a sale. I was in transition after being the president. It was my first experience of the challenge of working with so many personalities on the board, the employees, and the venture culture. I was in process, still asking myself what my purpose was in the life I was to lead. During my break time, I'd write profusely about leadership, and I remember taking one of my long book pieces to Rajmohan Gandhi. I also remembered that I found myself not ready to publish because my goal was to write to learn. I clearly had not learned enough. So, I abandoned that book. It is still in my drawer!

A few months later, I woke up from a torturous dream, and one word rose to my conscious mind—Cause. An aha moment! It seemed so simple. That the reason why companies failed was not that they chose the wrong strategy or had the wrong leaders. It was because they lost their identity, their reason for existence. Hence, they lost their identity and then lost their way. It all seemed so simple and elegant. Without aligning to a cause greater than yourself, you find yourself aligning to your ego and framing your mind around you. Without that north star that takes you and your company away from the narcissistic views, you are cursed to a journey of greed, ambition, and self-referenced desire. Further, I saw the direct relationship in the personal transformation of Gandhi, who let a cause find and inhabit him, and how he changed the world forever. So, I had found my own recipe for seeing the world of business. I found a way to live alongside the rough and sharp edges of business while keeping my own self intact.

Remember my father telling me that I was not ready? I knew then that I was ready to take on my purpose of transforming my world because I seemed to have practiced my own personal transformation.

I then began to build a framework to transform organizations through leaders who chose a cause to transform themselves. This framework helped several companies and helped my coaching business take off. CEO coaching had not developed or been a career yet.

That question of Cause accompanied me for years, until ten years later, I was asked to transform a US$11 billion not-for-profit healthcare organization, using these practiced principles. I used these frameworks and philosophies to design and structure the business based upon an organizational cause greater than itself. I joined the organization as an executive and led it through a fifteen-year transformation journey alongside eight thousand employees. It was a wonderful journey of serving healthcare and its members as well as honing my theories and principles.

I tell this story to illustrate the power of just one question from an insight-centered person to another who was ready for such a realization. It is also an illustration of the transportability and agility of a cause framework that started from my father, who fashioned his life around Gandhi's philosophy, and how it reappeared in my mind through Gandhi's grandson. Causes are taken while missions are given. But causes visit you for you to take them. They are all around us, waiting for us to be vessels of transformation and insight.

What if the Mahatma Gandhi, who is the father of modern India, were able to return to our present-day business environment? What would he think? First of all, would the automated AI-generated systems reject his resume application? Let us revisit his transformation prior to his impact on our world via a cause to free the Indians from British rule.

How to Ignite Your Inner Innovator

There is a moment of crisis that comes before failure—a subtle unraveling where people begin to lose more than just their jobs. They lose their identity, their sense of purpose, their understanding of what truly matters. This erosion doesn't happen through dramatic failures or strategic missteps, but through a gradual disconnection from one's core reason for existing.

Most people live trapped in a cycle of external expectations. They craft perfect professional personas, build impressive LinkedIn profiles, and chase career milestones without ever asking the most crucial question: What would not exist if I did not exist? It's a question that stops most people in their tracks, revealing the hollow performance of modern professional life.

The real power of innovation does not come from skills or strategies but from discovering a cause greater than oneself. Consider Sara

Blakely, the creator of Spanx. Her focus was a smother look under clothing for women. Before that, she was a door-to-door fax machines salesperson. Her transformation wasn't about acquiring skills but about embracing a vision that transcended her current limitations. Starting her business with five thousand dollars, she is now the envy of others and a force of her own.[1]

Organizations typically approach potential through a narrow lens. They analyze markets, assess capabilities, and try to optimize performance. But they miss the fundamental truth: A genuine cause is the ultimate organizational force. It cuts through market noise, transforms individual potential, and creates momentum that traditional strategies cannot replicate.

The distinction between a mission and a cause is critical. A mission is assigned, external, and temporary. A cause is chosen, deeply personal, and eternal. "Make retirement money" is a mission. "Feed my children in body and soul" is a cause. One is a transaction; the other is a transformation.

Now is the time to bring clarity to your dream, not to be bogged down by reality. If we rely on a mission to be handed to us, it will be narrow, instructional, and will inspire us to dig bunkers to hide from the oncoming Gen AI invasion. But a cause to elevate our community of AI-enabled innovators powered by their true inner selves might just be more exciting.

Mission Versus Cause

1. A mission is given, while a cause springs from within oneself.

2. A mission is a short-term action, while a cause is an everlasting theme that guides you.

3. A mission has organizational implications, while a cause has personal implications if it is not followed.

4. A mission is established for you, while a cause is taken by you.

5. A mission imposes a will upon you, while a cause brings out your will.

6. A mission is clear in its economics, while an effective cause has meaning and economic potency.

In the era of Gen AI, your competitive advantage lies in your ability to have a reason for existence that machines cannot replicate. Gen AI is designed to understand tasks but lacks empathy, purpose, and the ability to dream beyond its training data. An innovator's true power comes from serving a higher calling—challenging the status quo while simultaneously creating value.

Historical figures like Gandhi, Martin Luther King, Jr., and Nelson Mandela didn't start with a perfect plan. They started with a cause that was bigger than themselves. Their personal transformations became the catalysts for societal change. They understood that to truly innovate, they must first be willing to be transformed.

This transformation requires a different approach:

- Listen deeply to the world around you.
- Document stories of suffering and potential.
- Stay connected to your dreams before getting lost in logistics.
- Be prepared to commit fully.
- Communicate your vision with passion and authenticity.

The most profound innovation doesn't come from what you can do, but from why you are willing to do it. It's about finding that intersection between your unique capabilities and the world's most pressing needs.

Ask yourself the ultimate question: What would I be willing to die for? If you can answer that, you've found your cause. Now, live for it.

In an age of Gen AI and constant disruption, your greatest innovation will be your ability to still remain fundamentally human—to dream, to feel, to transform, and to serve a purpose greater than yourself. Many of us may be so enamored with this new "best AI assistant" we have all day and night that we become as robotic as possible, forgetting ourselves in the new expectations set by the machine. We now say "lol" instead of laugh out loud because we document our reaction. We post photos of our meals and have AI analyze them, but I wonder if we chose the specific meal because it could get more "likes." I know of young adults who chat with their dates by using ChatGPT to test their responses. Many have used GPT for counseling their own mental health. Others have used it for guiding their divorce proceedings and their moods through tough moments. On the one hand, it's gratifying to see that, given the difficulty in getting direct help for these needs, there is AI help. On the other hand—What the hell is going on that we are okay with a machine guiding our own mental states?

In my various keynotes, audience members often ask questions. Cause is a very attractive subject that spurs queries. Many ask me, "How do I find a cause?" I have several responses. But the one overall message is that if you are not awake to the present, feeling its various joys and injustices, it's not easy to notice a cause when it visits you. Once in my travels, I approached a Maori chief after her presentation and asked a very direct philosophical question. I asked, "What do you do when the butterflies visit you?"

She awakened with a shock and a smile and said, "Oh my! Well, you stand still!"

To her and to me, the butterflies symbolized insights that visit us daily, but we seldom notice because we are tuned away from our receptors, that is, our senses, our nervous system, our mind. We focus on our phone or other forms of mindless entertainment or news. These are designed to elicit preprogrammed responses from you. You think they are conversing with you, but they are talking to their advertisers about how many eyeballs they gathered and for how long.

Causes that yearn for your genius are all around you to take. When you make a decision to take a cause, things happen to encourage you forward. You see people who notice you and help. You find new ideas to fix the flaws. You sometimes find solutions in odd places. However, you also find that it's very difficult to solve, and you see so many obstacles. I have finally realized why it gets so difficult. It's because it's cognitively stimulating and is the preprocessing needed for you to live a better cognitive life filled with insights, and not AI machine-led but AI machine-enabled. In knowing your cause, you make Gen or Agentic AI an instrument of your purpose, not the purpose itself.

The journey of an innovator is not about being the best. It's about being the most authentically committed to a cause that matters. However, having a cause and seeking to fight for it is only one ingredient in the flywheel one needs to gain insight and the aha. Two other components are needed to unlock insight.

ACTION LEARNING

As an inner innovator in an AI era, you differentiate yourself by having a reason for existence as opposed to machines that augment the current status quo. You stand for a transformation, and you deploy AI. You have a reason for being. Mission, which is your why, is less relevant or is subordinate to the cause. Find that cause and ask yourself whether you are ready to create the scaffolding to attain it. Ask yourself whether you are willing to bet your plans on it. If it is something you are willing to be fired for, then work for it.

Communicate and ask others for the same commitment even though they will ask the expected questions: "How can I commit when I have yet to see what the objectives are and what the outcome is?" Remind them that as innovators they define future reality, not others. Remind them that they must train their minds to see through the walls of computational limitations and that without them there is no direction.

Uncover who you consider the customers of your cause and discover how far we have to travel. Know that, most probably, our current tools cannot get us there, and new competencies have to be realized. Get them there with AI as an accelerator. If you are not cause driven, you fall prey to fitting into the current narrative. The story that started the chapter is an example of this— my parents did not see the future but imagined it and then fought to manifest it. I watched them talk to other parents about the work they were doing. They would always say that what they did was not for them but for their children and the future. This was not rational. There was no evidence about the future and yet, they saw it to be as they wanted. They were compassionate to each other and not rational. AI is being used without any compassion and does the rational thing. Avoid this kind of blindness. There will be time, in this process of manifesting your future, where AI will be the tool for rational, computational actions.

Just start your transformation. Asking permission or explaining yourself will do some good. But it's asking before you transform yourself, and it will weaken your cause. Show others what they should challenge themselves with.

Avoid the grand idea or the common solution. Spend time listening and telling stories and documenting stories of suffering or injustices you witness. As an innovator, find your inspiration first and don't allow your brain to dive into all the "hows," as this will lead you to avoid engaging. Stay with your dreams at this time.

Innovator, create the conditions for your cause!

CHAPTER 8

Insight: Configure Your Craft

Early in my life, I was at the University of Oregon studying AI/ computer science. The world was opening up to new forms of fun and new ways to challenge students. I came from Singapore, and I seemed to be a pioneer in Oregon, where people seldom saw an Indian-Singaporean who spoke the King's English.

After I completed my first two years as an undergraduate, Dr. Wong, a prominent doctor in Singapore, asked to speak with me about his then seventeen-year-old son who was considering studying finance at Oregon. He wanted me to support and mentor his son. I met Russel, an intriguing young man, who asked to join me in the United States. We flew together via Hawaii. He took his high-power camera to the beach, while I carried my art pads to draw.

We became fast and close friends in Oregon. Russel continued to explore photography even though he continued in finance. He would hang around the famous Hayward Field to take photographs of the runners. In those days, we could run around the track without restrictions. There, Russel took photos of famous runners from Nike. He asked them for permission to take their photos and then gave them his photos. In that way, he built relationships with the athletes. After a while, they asked him to show Nike his photos. He did, and they told him that if they chose his shots, he would get rewarded with a free pair of Nike shoes. He got the shoes; but even better—he got the cover of the prestigious magazine.

From Talent to Craft

After Russel's graduation, he decided to pursue his work in fine arts in Los Angeles. In LA, he hustled for gigs from agents. He would ask agents for an opportunity to photograph anyone. One agent told him about one actor who was challenging. According to this agent, this young actor was known for not keeping his appointments. Russel agreed to take the job. He sat in his studio and waited. The actor did not turn up for hours. Then came a call.

The actor, named Robert Downey Jr., called and asked Russel if he had food. Russel said yes without admonishing Robert for his lateness. Russel cooked lunch for Robert at his studio, and they ate together. There, he learned about Robert's dream of becoming a great actor. They forged a trusting relationship, and this became one of Russel's big breaks. Russel realized that to be an outstanding photographer, he needed to research and understand the desires and dreams of his subjects.

Russel, while at New York University for the summer, was invited to a party where Jackie Chan and Michelle Yeoh were present. He took photos of them. As was his custom, Russel initiated a conversation with his subjects and made an impression on them. Jackie asked Russel why he didn't work in Hong Kong rather than work for Americans. Jackie invited Russel to Hong Kong. Russel accepted the invitation. In Hong Kong, Jackie mentored Russel and helped him establish himself in connection with Jackie's franchise of *Rush Hour* movies and others. Subsequently, Michelle Yeoh opened doors for Russel with her *Crouching Tiger* movie and others. Russel became the photographer of these stars.[1]

He is now the chosen celebrity photographer for Jackie Chan, Michelle Yeoh, and famous jazz greats. He loves movies, jazz, race cars, and other interesting subjects. Photographing subjects that align with his interests is his passion in action. He knows that his research skills and passions power his photography. Russel tells me that he does not see himself as a photographer. He is a skilled researcher. He is curious and always generating new ideas. He is relentless with his pursuit of the next shot, but he studies the subject intensely, and that's what makes his subjects curiously attracted to him. He seems not to chase the shot; he seems to be inhabiting the areas that his subjects are passionate about, and they seem to recognize that Russel is like them. Inspired.

He loves imperfections, and thus dislikes Gen AI photo enhancement. When we met in Singapore, he told me about the concept of wabi-sabi.[2] This wisdom finds beauty in imperfection. I could really see, in his art form, how he embraces the natural beauty of imperfection and expresses it in his work. He reminded me that a better camera does not create a better photographer. Nothing more. It's never the tech but the person behind the camera who must push through and express the genius within.

When I asked Russel how he finds that perfect shot every time, he told me he does not know. When I pushed for more, he revealed that the shot finds him. What the heck does that mean? I can only interpret that to mean that he has built a recipe he uses to create the meal of his expression—the photograph. And he awaits the echo of his hard work to appear. He has honed his insight and instinct through practice. He seems to be able to use his insight of the subject to find the perfect shot seemingly on demand.

He is now a celebrity even in front of the camera. If you watch *Crazy Rich Asians*, you will come to a moment where a character, played by Ronnie Cheng, demands that his family take promo photos. He calls out to his photographer. That is Russel Wong in a cameo. He is so famous, he played himself in the movie.

Consider that Russel found his craft not by accident but through hard work, hustling, and building his recipe. He has talent, but from the age of seventeen, he dedicated work and time to his skills and developed them. Skills aside, he designed his craft as a combination of skills, his ability to interact with humans, his inspired research capability, his broad curiosity, his assertive selling, his camera skills, and his own unique business model.

Russel learned to get that second meeting with his prospects. That's why he would bring the photographs to his clients as gifts, knowing that many times, his clients never received the photographs that landed in *Time* or *Vogue*. Many well-known personalities never received their own copies because the magazines owned them. Russel always got them their own photos. They always remembered his unique approach. Russel built an identity via practiced action. He built his own craft based on a recipe:

1. It's not about the photograph; it's about the story told. Be a storyteller or story maker.

2. It's not about getting to the shot; it's about researching the subject and then letting the shot arrive. It's about knowing the reason for your work.

3. It's about practicing the art. Relentless practice.

4. Get to the second meeting to understand the subject. Always come back.

5. Be intensely curious and research obsessively before the shoot. Care enough to know the story behind the story.

To me, Russel is forever that innocent seventeen-year-old I met but one who is now incredibly more talented because of the years he suffered through to gain experience. He laughed at me during our last meeting when I asked him questions, trying to understand how he developed his craft. He laughed and told me he is not a deconstructive thinker like me. He told me he is pure instinct.

I explained to him, justifying my approach, that what comes naturally to him is a result of years of perfecting his recipe for his craft. It is not a definable process because it was forged and intertwined with his experiences, his business model, and his innate ability to find the insight in his subjects and prepare them to appear in his shot. It is a craft that cannot be brought to life through AI. It has soul because he prepares his subjects by preparing himself for them.

In simple terms, working on your craft gives you a window into the sight of your mind.

Jon Batiste, the famous music director for the *Late Show with Stephen Colbert*, visited the *Late Show* in 2024. He was a guest talking about his new endeavors. Stephen asked him if he was aware of leaders who would enter a room and bring oxygen with them, filling the room with new energy and making others want to do the work for this person. In other words, they wanted to be their best-performing self for this leader. Who would that be? Batiste responded with powerful comments about Stevie Wonder. He described the energy of seeing a human being and an artist synthesized as one when the artist's life and values align with their art. He said he felt this before Stevie even touched the instrument.

Do you know how that feels? Have you experienced such sacredness that took a lifetime to express? That is your craft expressed. It arrives before you even perform.

I love to draw, I love to sing, I love to write, and I love to watch great acting. I'm a performance artist, and I love to keynote. My entire craft is expression. It's just that simple.

Gen AI and Your Craft

Now look at the latest in creative expression tools provided by NVIDIA with audio AI Fugatto.[3] One can create sounds and blend them into audio in ways previously unimaginable. The relentless use of these special effects can be transformative. What does it do to the craft you are developing? How do you develop a recipe of skills to combine them into a craft that will stand against such delivery?

Amateurs will produce music and video and stories with prompt generators. Professionals may up their game even more with such tools. Then there is the group in between. What happens to their innovation mind? Does it deteriorate or elevate or both, meaning certain portions of our capabilities decay because we never use them due to tools like Fugatto? Others are enhanced. In all ways, the experts have trained their minds to elevate the tools. The amateurs will decay portions of their minds in this process.

What is your craft, which is what gives you a lens into your inner innovator? As you engage with your own form of self-expression, you will find the way into your innovative self. Think of yourself as a chef in training to find your voice in the meals you create. A cook makes a meal while a chef creates an experience unique to the brand they live and identify by. A chef never blames his ingredients for the meal. The chef uses the same ingredients combined in a rehearsed and highly trained way to produce a unique concoction that is unforgettable. And many times, it can be replicated only through the magic of experience.

Work is not usually your craft. You adapted your personal skills, which are ingredients, to engage with your work. You form your craft only after some quiet practice, introspection, and suffering through experimentation.

As the chef, your life is a story or a narrative. The meal symbolizes that story, symbolizes that experience, and tells that story. And so should anything you make or design. Your work is the meal you offer others. They should stand in line to watch you work and enjoy every bite of the outcomes. That is not machine-readable. That's what I'm talking about when I say that your practiced craft can meet any circumstance.

How Does Insight Come from Your Craft?

What you provide to your world, that which uniquely defines a recipe of your great skills and talents, gives you a lens to view the world differently than others. That's why Russel gets the best shots in six clicks. He is known for taking longer to setup than actually shooting the photos. As an innovator, you translate what you experience through this lens. If your craft lens is underdeveloped, your view inward is less clear, and you will have to find other ways to discover insight. The more you practice your inspired craft, the more you see inside and to your inner voice. That voice has been clouded by the external notices that are loud and, frankly, unproductive.

Howard Schultz was a coffee buyer when he stumbled on his insight of Starbucks while buying coffee in Europe. His trigger came when he watched customers sitting outside enjoying their coffee. His craft was not buying coffee. He was a student of behavior and markets.

In fact, he did not start Starbucks. He bought the company from its founders, who then moved to Peet's Coffee. Howard was more interested in espresso and wanted to introduce that to the American public. What was his craft that powered the insight to be the daring market creator he is? Now with AI in the mix, what craft is essential for an innovator to succeed?

These are questions I don't have answers to. I refuse to talk of the predictions that are just wrong. But I have insight into this question.

What I do know is that you must understand your craft—what you are and do better than anyone else. You must know your own combination of skills and talents that push you to the top of the pyramid. What is your recipe that brings out your inner innovator?

With this as your lens, you can observe the momentum of markets and communities. You can watch what people do in your chosen community and use your lens to see what is coming that your community cannot yet see.

A Lesson in Tradecraft

When I was in grade school and high school, I really wanted to be in the sciences. In Singapore, it was something of a rite of passage to be a science student. Somehow, in my head and the heads of others around me, the people in my community thought more highly of the sciences than of the arts. So, I fell prey to that bias.

One powerful thing was that the education I received was very balanced with both literature and mathematics. Now I cherish the broad education and the caring instruction I received in my early years. It was tough times for my lower-middle-class family; we struggled as immigrants in Singapore. I recall the private sacrifices that only a tall drink and old friends will be able to draw out of me.

My parents slept overnight in the street to get me into a private school filled with rich kids. I knew the difference between me, who had one set of shoes, and those who were driven to school in their limos.

I always wondered what I would be when I grew up. I thought about being a structural engineer. I loved mathematics and physics. But I also developed an artistic side. I was an above-average artist with watercolors and drawing, and I loved to sing and play the guitar.

I could not afford a new guitar, but I had a hand-me-down that worked. Later, I purchased a new one, which I still have today. I carried it on my plane flights and used it throughout my life.

But I really believed that the arts would be too difficult and that the sciences would be more reliable. What if my creativity suddenly stopped? What would I do? So, I continued to pursue the sciences. I let my art and music take second place while still playing daily and dreaming of being a star, even as I did my work as a computer scientist and worked to become a businessman.

The irony of all this was that I was not the best computer scientist. The one thing I could count on was not my science but my recipe of science and art. All those years I was honing my own unique, brazen quality. It was not that I was science or art; it was that I viewed the world through expressive, innovative lenses. My creativity would never stop. I was an overindulgent innovator using my media mindset, thinking in music, movies, and innovative terms.

The best computer scientists were those who were hyper capable of inventing, writing, and creating algorithms that stunned others. I, on the other hand, had the skills to educate others on complex algorithms, market them into the minds of customers, and creatively design the right frameworks to win in markets. I decided my craft was this combination. I won others over with my passion for expression—speaking, entertaining but educating, and most of all, finding innovative ways to get through the mental clutter.

I became a marketer, then CEO, then board member. The irony is that all I loved to do on the side formed the ingredients that created the recipe for the craft I now inhabit.

That is the message I share with you about finding your craft. What you do is not your craft. It is your job. Your craft, if you actually plan it, can be the unique recipe of ingredients you provide, that you offer to others for them to pay you, enjoy you, and admire you. It is the source of insight.

Your abilities are those things you are good at, but they are not your competencies. Your competencies are what make you stand above others; they are what you are so good at, in combination, that makes you unreachable by others.

This journey of discovery through your competencies is one of the greatest challenges of your life. When I listen to others who tell me what I do well, it bothers me. Mostly, they only know a part of what I know of myself. This journey seems endless, but that's because it is within you.

ACTION LEARNING

Journal your thoughts.

1. List your top five capabilities that you believe could form the ingredients of your craft.

1. _____

2. _____

3. _____

4. _____

5. _____

2. Weight from one to five the level of dominance each one of these capabilities has in comparison to others in your world.

1. _____

2. _____

3. _____

4. _____

5. _____

3. Take the top three of them and combine them into what you believe you can offer to any innovation endeavor that you are a part of today.

_____

_____

_____

4. List the top five trends that you believe are happening in your world today.

1. _____

2. _____

3. _____

4. _____

5. _____

5. Create a table of two columns. The first column will be called trends, and the second column will be called momentum. Write the trend that you believe is occurring that will last more than five years. Then write the momentum underlying the trend that powers the trend. Some of the trends may be powered by the same momentum driver.

TRENDS	MOMENTUM

6. Look at underlying momentum drivers that are like currents in the ocean and drive more than one trend, that is, more than one wave.

_____

_____

_____

7. Identify a momentum driver and a craft that you believe you have that you could use to accelerate that momentum driver. Or create a story that allows you to take advantage of the change that is about to arrive. Practice this regularly.

_____

_____

_____

CHAPTER 9

Insight: Unlock the Community

Meet late Professor Bala Balachandran. He was my closest confidant and mentor. For more than twenty-five years, Uncle Bala, as he liked to be called, was a renowned Professor of Accounting Information and Management at the Kellogg School of Management at Northwestern University. I met him when we were both keynote speakers at a conference called CAM-I (Consortium of Advanced Management-International), run by my other good friend and colleague Ashok Vadgama.

I watched Bala as he mesmerized the audience by giving life to the esoteric topic of activity-based costing for organizational performance management. At that time, I was president of a fledgling startup called ABC Technologies, which sold software in the same field.

Bala took to me quickly, and he decided (after a very detailed interrogation) that he would partner with me and my organization. We then formed a bond to build activity-cost management as an industry, which was formed by great leaders such as Professor Robert Kaplan and Dr. Robin Cooper.

My friendship with Bala blossomed, and we worked jointly on articles and teaching at Kellogg on cost and performance management for more than twelve years. There, I watched executives and MBA students study under and learn from the wisdom of Bala. He was more than an educator. He could engage prime ministers and students equally. He was a performer of sorts. He lived out his values in everything he did. He was a disciplined learner and listener. He worshiped his higher power but knew he had to do the hard work.

Bala decided to retire at sixty-five. But the world lost an educator only for a short while. Then one day, Bala called me and told me he was going to design and build a new school in his hometown, where his mother lived. He wanted to pay it forward. He wanted to build the unbuildable—a university that rivaled others in the world. An MBA-only college where values drove the work and where students would have the ability to execute on their dreams using an eighteen-month MBA curriculum. He asked for my support. I gave it without question and offered myself as an advisor.

I quickly came to realize that I was not doing him a favor. He was doing one for me. The list of advisors consisted of spectacular leaders who were prominent thought leaders in the world; many were originally from India, but the list included many others such as Professor Philip Kotler, founder of modern marketing, and the late Ratan Tata, chair of the Tata conglomerate. They all saw what Bala was doing to build for the community he cherished.

From age sixty-five until eighty-four, when he passed away, Bala led the enterprise as chairperson and dean emeritus of the Great Lakes Institute of Management[1] in Chennai, India. He was awarded Padma-Shri, the highest honor in India, by the Prime Minister of

India for his contributions to his community. Uncle Bala was a prominent developer and accelerator of innovation for both the United States and India.

I had a front row seat to his life performance. I spoke to him every other day for more than twenty years. I can say very clearly that he was not about ego or ambition. He was about community. His inspiration was to bring new ideas to communities and to develop a platform that others could use as a springboard for their own climbs. His insight was powered by what he saw as the missing elements of education; this was his unique contributive recipe to MBA education. His community consisted of all those who sought to learn with humility. Bala was a force to reckon with. He was competitive and relentless. He never stopped building his dream, and he always brought others along with him. He created wealth. He was a teacher and an entertainer. He loved people who learn and innovate.

I visited him often to catch his energy and share our mutual dreams. Then his health started to fail him, and I wanted to see him. But he was too busy receiving his visitors. He would tell me to visit after others left so that he could be with me in private. I did not get that chance. I am told that in his last days, he would still get out of bed to catch my call, never telling me that the time was arriving.

In Chennai, at Great Lakes Institute of Management, a statue memorializes his influence and presence. Students speak of him as a hero. I know him as an inner innovator powered by his own unique and essential gifts—his insight and his ability to build scaffolding for his community to build upon. He was my friend.

Insight is a function of service to the community. If, instead, we innovators call the people we serve customers, we can become trapped in a frame that is unbecoming. Innovators like to transform communities. We enjoy changing our world. Transforming customers from non-buyers to buyers is, frankly, boring and pedestrian. The great innovators move mountains by moving communities. Think of the great business leaders who found communities to serve and found insight in the process of providing services or products that captured the imagination of these communities. Steve Jobs found creatives. Elon Musk found car enthusiasts who were energy conscious. Gandhi found freedom seekers who became freedom nonviolent fighters. Who is your community? Who do you wish to free from tyranny? Some are lost in the tyranny of the present status quo. Others are trapped in their own minds.

Innovators powered by insight build scaffolding that the members of the community will climb. The mobile phone existed before the iPhone, but the iPhone was the human productivity platform. Why? The community consisted of zealots. Elon Musk had zealots following his ideas as well. They were patient and believed in his design for the future.

What is the difference between customers and community? Just words? Customers are addressed by value propositions. You sell them your value, and they pay a price for it. They get a benefit from taking the benefits minus the price they paid.

A community is about values proposition. They pay a price to join your movement and share your expressed values and transform themselves and others in the ever-expanding community.

The values proposition is what innovators believe in and is how they manifest their belief in their creations. More communities are buying products and services based on what they see as aligned beliefs. AI has no belief and seeks only to replicate your beliefs and mine. AI has no community and is trying to swallow the world of the output of communities. AI cannot empathize with those who suffer from the tyranny of the present and move them to the dreams of their future.

AI can only respond when prompted and cannot solve problems unprompted. But these agents focus on jobs to be done and do not move communities forward. Inner innovators find communities.

ACTION LEARNING

Journal your thoughts.

1. Which community do you enjoy? Which community is suffering from pain points to be solved?

_____

_____

_____

2. Can you see a future state that is transformative for these communities? List them.

_____

_____

_____

3. Describe these communities in nontraditional ways. Don't use personas or segments like we always do. Use the habits, behaviors, and values of these communities to discuss how you enable these habits further.

_____

_____

_____

4. What inspires your work in these communities? In what ways do they evolve when you exist? What would not happen if you did not exist?

_____

_____

_____

CHAPTER 10

Build Scaffolding: The Language of Insight

My dog, a beautiful short-haired mini dachshund, never stopped loving me throughout her life. I miss her every day when I see other dogs or when I hear a bark. She left an indelible mark on my life and changed it forever—and not just because she was a loving and caring friend. She was also a highly intelligent species and was a copilot to all my thoughts and feelings.

She intuitively anticipated all of my needs and also knew how to show love and loyalty beyond any human I could ever meet. Her capacity to bring human and animal together was unmatchable.

She showed me how to love unconditionally. I knew she was more intelligent than many humans around her. But we define intelligence in a unique way in AI. It is computational, and this ability to translate everything machines witness into compute parameters and then translate it back is not the same as what my dog did. She did not compute but merged computational mathematics and her inner being to solve issues.

She could find a frisbee in midair. She could identify a squirrel and scare it with an attack. She could uncover a rat in the backyard even without seeing it. She could also understand the humans around her to gauge a threat or know when she would be petted. Machines cannot predict this far and wide, even after all these years of training.

My dog lost her sight from illness and found it difficult to maneuver around the house if junk was in her way, and she would bang into it. But if I placed her in the backyard to do her business, she would find the edge of the grass and triangulate to find the safest center of the garden, do her business, and then return to the edge where she would travel until she found my voice.

She lost her abilities but created new approaches she used to exist. This is how innovators motivated from within create scaffolding to climb repeatedly and for others to follow. Scaffolding is the second part of how insight-powered AI-enabled innovators function. They practice the power of insight in all that they do, but they then move to act upon their ideas and create that which is yet to be dreamed. This chapter and the next one delve into the tools to build scaffolding once insight is generated.

Machines have spent a lifetime getting deep learning algorithms that emulate the brain to get the visual capacity that dogs cultivate. Dogs had this at birth, practiced these abilities, and built it to adulthood.

So, are dogs and other animals more intelligent than AI machines, and are we barking up the wrong tree defining intelligence so narrowly to focus on brain functions? I say yes. I believe we are mistaking the brain for the integrative nature of intelligence. Dogs prove my thesis that we seem to speak of artificial general intelligence without appreciating other intelligences like animals. Our world is populated with various intelligences yet to be understood.

We have used language interpretations and transformation as our inroad into Gen AI currently, but we have other methods deployed like deep learning methods to understand vision and sound. We are getting there and spending incredible compute capabilities to muster the capacity of a dog who does her business in the garden.

Insight, the aha, as I discuss in this book, pays homage to the belief that we are more than our thoughts secreted from our brains. We are our innovative ideas in action found in our minds. But language, being one path to intelligence copied by AI now, demands that we know how to use it to build teams and bring action to the work we all do.

Language and prompts are now in the forefront of the AI revolutions. Everyone now thinks that the prompt defines the outcome. And language is the power trigger to intelligence. Given this, inner innovators must learn it as a tool for transforming people, teams, and our work.

My dog captured the entire spectrum of senses, cognition, and her historical biology to be my best friend. Further, dogs can also measure the intent of the human, not just the output of the human. Machines are not able to do this. Yet, if we are to master the machine, we must be more like my dog than the machine. We must integrate all our capabilities to render a future view to create. We must muster language, prompt our teams, and also imagine the future we see beyond the present and then go make that happen.

Remember, the use of transformative language is only one form of getting to the heartbeat of innovation. Accordingly, we are motivated by words, and understanding how to prompt ourselves and others as though we ourselves are LLMs is interesting. We create a language semantic field in our minds that collects all our experiences and the words and movies we create in a big database in our minds. It is an almost circular field of words and pictures with meaning attached to each that we use as a database to protect us and also motivate us. With the right prompt, we can draw from this field to excel or be stopped.

My dog had her own field of semantic and syntactic information. She also knew when to do standard things and when to act beyond her own thinking and take the necessary risks to advance forward. She drew on her history, her own view of the world, and also something more: her own insight, which she trusted if given the chance.

This chapter focuses on innovative language that you can practice to enable yourself to reach new heights of transformation and not be imprisoned by the cages of the status quo. But the language is not just spoken—it is action. Like my dog who notices everything, she can hear my words, smell her direction, hear for miles, and also watch my actions. This is the language I am asking you to consider.

Machines cannot understand intent. They can, so far, only diagnose words, videos, and photos. Mind you, they are fabulous at interpreting your intent but not like humans. This chapter speaks of innovation language—not just words, but using all the facets of your cognition, your senses, your biology, and your humanity, to lead yourself and others. Just as my dog can rest next to me in a normal daily routine and also hunt for badgers in the field in full transformative engagement, navigating with ease terrain she has never experienced before, we must be able to live in both worlds.

But for now, let's discuss how words used in language (particularly English) can define your inner innovator and allow it to emerge for others.

I have defined inner innovators as people who are AI-enabled, not AI-obsessed, and who lead with insight-powered capabilities.

In chapter 2, I discussed the differences between status quo thinking and transformative thinking. I talked about how one and the other live in separate worlds of sorts, but that the power of an inner innovator is the skill to traverse both of these worlds, moving from broad thinking and design to tight operating actions. This ability to move in between both these worlds is rare, a skill of the future, and fundamental to designing and building the future yet to be experienced.

If you think too long and never act, you are a dreamer. If you act without dreaming, you are without purpose. I mean to say that transformative innovators sometimes lack the ability to bring their ideas into common understanding and actual work to be completed. Status quo innovators know that they must act but seldom design the new world for the future. The inner innovator knows how to train their team to know the difference between these two seemingly opposite approaches to leadership. These approaches seem to be almost polar opposites but can be carefully woven into a tapestry of options for great innovators.

Similarly, the great innovators transport themselves and their innovation teams between living within the status quo and moving to innovation speed and language, guiding their teams to achieve the appropriate mission. This type of leadership is not easily trained or attainable. It is a living practice for the innovator to master every day of their innovation lives.

Status quo commonly uses language that reduces risk and streamlines activities and thus removes redundancies. Innovation language increases risk and opportunity accordingly and thus increases redundancies.

To Prompt or Not to Prompt?

Have you noticed that we humans are similar to LLM containers? We too have developed large models that connect all our experiences and learnings into an equation with billions of parameters to assess and engage in our world. In a way, we speak to other humans who have their own LLMs in their brains, and we prompt them with questions. In certain situations, we see common ground, and in others we see otherwise. But we function off of prompts just like Gen AI does.

But we use semantic (words and meaning) as well as syntactic (words only) models to work, while LLMs currently use syntactic connections. Language prompts serve to direct our thoughts and feelings. We are influenced deeply by language, visual prompts, and emotional prompts. In fact, we each have unique thoughts daily. On average, we have about six thousand thoughts per day. So, we not only prompt others, we are also prompting our own inner self. A study published in *Nature*[1] calculates this. But it concludes this by measuring the number of transitions thinking subjects had per minute. The higher the neuroticism of the subject, the higher the number of thoughts. How many of the thoughts you have per day are transformative or status quo related?

AI and Prompting

These days, we have learned to prompt our AI machines to ask them to produce whatever we desire. We ask them to summarize an article or draft an email we want to develop or refine. We have learned that a prompt to an AI engine, be it ChatGPT or Gemini, delivers results that depend on the specificity of our language. We have witnessed an explosion of courses on prompt engineering that has created an entirely new field of study.

I think this will evolve and transform as technology advances and does away with prompting altogether. You now can, for example, specify a goal, and AI agents, with multiple prompts built into them, will execute your desired goals.

What I see as ironic is that we have used language to enhance our lives for centuries, but little has been done to understand how we use language to motivate humans to be "prompted" to increase their higher capacities. We speak of motivation, but we lose ourselves in broad terms of comfort and use language that is basic BS that conforms to norms instead of taking us to a higher place of innovative action.

Change Your Innovation Language; Change Your Mind

Part of building a scaffolding in the minds of others you want to influence and lead is choosing the language you use to awaken their cognitive capacity. We already know enough about how humans respond to particular contexts and meaning. Watch the battle scene in the movie *Braveheart* where the leader motivates his troops to die for their cause. Words and contexts always motivate others.

What about when we want to help others go beyond the pedestrian notions of Gen AI doing everything and humans finding the higher form of insight?

George Orwell, in his book *1984*, writes about a world with a dominant culture that controls everything, including how its citizens think. The language used by the culture in this book is called Newspeak, and it was created to ensure that words control minds. The slogans of the dystopian world are WAR IS PEACE, FREEDOM IS SLAVERY, and IGNORANCE IS STRENGTH. The story of this controlled society is about how the dominant forces created a language that expresses the opposite of what is usually understood. This "doublespeak" language rules the operating culture, and everything is the opposite of what you say. What does that do to your mind, I wonder?

Further, the *1984* world is designed with four principles to control subjects: language is a tool for controlling minds, physical control is the threat, technology is the power, and wealth is the elite that rules while the poor are the subjects under control. There is no middle class, so one has only two choices in life. All this is done under the theme, "Big Brother Is Watching." This slogan from the book has crept into the common vernacular and is now a commonly used term.

Doublespeak is quite common in today's environments when leaders speak of ideas being important but punish new ideas. When a person says one thing but does the opposite, we see that the opposite is the truth. Doublespeak can be seen all around us; it is like a virus. This should scare any leader because *1984* is about a dominant authoritarian leadership. If this is evident in your life, you are living in a mental cage. You will not be able to innovate beyond the

AI machine unless you change and expand your language beyond the standard rule-following, risk-averse language. The most subtle and important conversation we should have centers on the use of language and the mental censorship that occurs with regard to innovative thinking and doing.

A Word About Innovation Language

Professor Lera Boroditsky at the University of San Diego is a long-time researcher in the field of language.[2] She has documented several ways in which language can shape thinking. Do words define us, or do we define words to represent our thoughts? This is an ongoing debate. Ample research has shown that our words define our thoughts and the thoughts of others. Language, according to Lera, guides our reasoning.

We know that how we understand our world is directly influenced by the language architecture we use; different architectures cause differences in our understanding of the world. In Lera's talks, she notes that many people in the West associate time with space using terms like "the hour is approaching," which is not shared by people who speak some other languages. People in some other countries have more defined categories for the colors; language is used to describe shades that express deeper considerations. Lera gives us a view into how language can shape thoughts, both your own and those of others, and how those thoughts lead to actions.

Consequently, those of us in the business of innovation must be aware of how the words we use to express our values and our intentions about innovation and transformation affect others. People process such words very differently. We also use metaphors, according to Lera, when we speak of things (e.g., accelerate this program or stop it in its tracks). These metaphors are chosen from a "wartime" era versus a "peacetime era," and they can evoke different pathways in our minds and in the minds of others.

So how do we, as innovators, avoid bringing only one kind of language format to the conforming and innovation endeavor? For many of us, there are two games in town. Operational efficiency, what I call conforming/status quo, and innovation leaps, which I call transformative. Are there two types of innovation language? Yes, there are. Do we stick to these lanes to create consistent messaging about action? If we stick, we will be stuck when we want to change. I propose that there are nuances in this conversation on innovation language and you do not have to be a linguist to communicate to the innovation and operational worlds around you.

Have you ever heard the phrase "the minute he opened his mouth"? That is the challenge, because how we speak and write determines the first impression and even triggers preconceived biases. How do we as innovators allow and encourage the dual language of status quo and transformation in our business and flow between operational language and innovation language without confusion and conflict? Many innovators choose one form of expression that probably gives listeners one form of impression and way of acting. But the nuance in innovation is that there is no one way to be an inspired inner innovator.

Sometimes we focus on operating effectively, while other times we dream about and design the future. Other times we are at a place in between, where we are creating the options for the present operational focus. This confuses everyone. Separating innovation and operating business in organizations has its merits, but separating language the same way creates silos and cultural islands. Bringing the language together and allowing for both operational and transformative language is a skill few have mastered. The ones who have mastered it have elevated their innovation effectiveness.

Use Language as a "Prompt" for Insight

Consider innovation as being organized into the following categories:

Conforming/status quo—where preserving the status quo is of paramount importance.

Transformative—where the incumbent does their thing while a new market is created alongside it, bringing ALL the customers to align with the new product or service while the market transforms.

Usually, a transformative innovation comes years after one prepares for it—the one that sees it before others and designs the new market or business model even when the current model does not support it. For example, Tesla was designing for self-driving cars years before the regulatory framework existed. In the 1980s, Intel was designing the new bus architecture prior to it becoming a standard, but they built it while they made it a standard. So those transformative innovations predicted a structural shift in customer values and designed for it.

Both of these categories require the use of unique language, but we tend to use language interchangeably between both categories. That is the problem. Apart from the fact that the English language has numerous gaps that impede its effectiveness, it is also filled with controversies and contradictions. Each of these two categories creates assumptions that are unique to each context. It's like using only prepositions while talking to a person who never uses prepositions. They will not understand you. When your language lacks clarity, you get compliance because others will follow what you say literally, but you will seldom get ingenious results. So when someone does not understand a game analogy, telling them to "get to the baseline" means nothing. The inner innovator in you should carefully deploy effective language.

Research has affirmed that teams who were influenced just before a test by specific language, movies, etc. that were focused on analytic thinking were more likely to respond with analytic examples and thoughts during the test.[3] Further, if the team was provided with strategic examples and stories before a test, they would respond with strategic responses. This research showed that the time needed to reconfigure a team's approach could be as short as five minutes before the meeting. This example is an amazing demonstration of the effect of recency of impact of language on the brain/mind.

Innovation is fueled by ideas. Your conforming/status quo brain is fueled by control systems that create conformity and allow for ideas within the bounds of allowed thought. So, anything beyond that swim lane is considered bad or out of step. But ideas cannot be controlled because they start and exist in our minds, not our brains. Try telling yourself not to think about any one particular thing, and it will never leave your mind. So, the belief that we can control how we think is partially false. We can manage our mind to ignore or acknowledge. We can control our brains in order to bring about conforming behaviors. Yet, I observe that leaders frequently tell people what to think and sometimes even how. This is the friend to the consistent and efficient brain but the enemy of the innovation mind.

The world of ideas is part of the world of innovation where we use language to fuel our new creations. There is always a time to focus after we brainstorm and get started producing one thing.

What language does one use to fuel ideas and to keep them coming while not affecting operational issues? The first language is one that encourages, collects, and responds to ideas. Leaders encourage everyone to contribute, assess, vote on, and create a pipeline of ideas that make things better, create new opportunities, or create breakthrough business models. Everyone is allowed into the network, and everyone has an equal vote or contribution. Ideas make the hierarchical world flat, and you are not judged by other prejudices but by the merit of your idea. The language of ideas with idea management is inclusive and diverse and gives voice to the voiceless or to those whose voice has been stolen by leaders who permit only work in silence.

Meanwhile, the operating part of our brain has a focus on conformity, efficiency, and repeatability. It wants to repeat processes continuously and produce the same outcomes over again. That part of our brain is threatened by anything out of the ordinary. It wants to remove randomness from the system. If you try to use that system to generate innovative ideas or talk about changing the entire model of work, it will be shocking.

How do we manage this as innovators? Why not create an alternative self-running system that is not threatened by these types of stories and can engage them without fear of reprisal? Why not think of the ways we might change and morph? This system is one that encourages a fascination with ideas and an idea management system and the careful use of language that enables such thoughts and actions. This must run parallel to the well-oiled and necessary operational brain with its efficient work system.

Let's consider the language most often used in these categories instead of using them interchangeably. These terms are simply examples; they are not definitive. The lesson here is to note the range in language use that can bring the best innovator self out of you and your team. How you respond determines the mental input and consequent outcomes. Here are some categories with examples to consider:

CONFORMING INNOVATION:
- Keep to the swim lanes.
- Engage the customer where they are.
- Design for the incremental move forward.
- Satisfy the current need and do not overshoot.
- Do not be ahead of the market because it is too early.
- Being early is as bad as being too late.
- Gain customers using the tools of today.
- Coopetition.
- Value proposition.
- Mission.
- No money, no mission.
- Boil the frog.
- Slay the dragon.
- Control the narrative.
- Dominate the market.
- Follow the mission.

- The status quo is the reason for work.
- Wartime metaphors (e.g., take it to the competition; conquer them; surround the market).
- Wartime language (e.g., capture share by undercutting, win customers).
- Hire the capable in the task at hand.
- Kill the competitor.
- Undercut the competitor.
- Acquire customers.
- Competition.
- Product–market fit.
- Speed to market.
- Principle of lower price and just enough value to win the bottom of the market.
- Destroy competitive pathways.
- Undercut markets.
- Cyclic changes in markets.
- Be first to market with product or service.
- Run to a mission.
- Hire those who bring skills to disrupt the competition.
- Momentum is gained after the growth phase.

TRANSFORMATIVE INNOVATION:

- Conquer the dreams of customers.
- Find new customers who are changing.
- Control the narrative.
- Be the leader for the new, transformed market.
- Leaders are rewarded and trained to uncover the new value proposition.

- Value proposition is based on the job to be done.

- Hire those who bring skills to transform the market and leave the competition to themselves.

- Create a new swim lane to purposefully capture the values of the customer.

- It's not about you; it's about transforming the injustice the customers face.

- The system must be transformed, and the people must transform to do it.

- Create new markets and be the leader so that you can change the system.

- Build the plane while flying the plane.

- The prepared mind prepares for structural change in our future.

- Enable the truth narrative of customers to lead our actions.

- Be the enabler or catalyst.

- Be and be perceived as the catalyst.

- Cause is transformation; money is money.

- Transform to a cause greater than ourselves.

- Momentum indicates the hidden movement of the market and drives the purchase. Momentum is found and then caught like a wave. In the beginning not the end.

- Align the values proposition as well as the value proposition; that is, the customer purchases the purpose of the company as well as the product.

- Leaders are rewarded for the values-driven approach to their team, which is transformational servant leadership. Hire those who display introspective, cause-driven competencies and bring a unique recipe to transform themselves while transforming the market.

Theory of Mind and Theory of Language

Many times in business, I've observed that leaders use language assuming others understand their colloquialisms. Others' thoughts, beliefs, desires, and intentions may not be like yours. That is what the theory of mind acknowledges—that it may be different.[4]

Here, the use of language should accommodate but also set the table for your innovation direction. Are you status quo or for transformative innovation or both? People talk to themselves regularly. Your inner innovator does not turn up unprompted. As humans we have the unique capacity to talk to ourselves. It's quite funny to catch myself talking to myself, especially when I forget that others are around me. When I realize this, I am quite embarrassed and wonder what I said! This is very much how we humans live.

AI machines don't have that problem or gift. The gift of introspective contemplation can be an asset or liability depending on our own language that we use to conjure our best or worst innovator self. Furthermore, our language spurs others we lead. But if we do not align our theory of mind with language, we create chaos in others' minds. To uncover your best transformative, confident, and insight-powered self, you must choose your language, especially the language you use on yourself first, then adapt that to others.

The term "selfing," used in mindfulness practice, argues that the overuse of identifying with oneself can create a world that traps us in our own thoughts. So, prompting your mind to be open to new ideas, to create the future and to train your own self to be introspective and not self-contained, is a necessary prompt for the inner innovator. You have to conjure the spell to bind your inner innovator to the goal, then bring out the best innovation selves in others and point them to the goal. If not, how can you bind others to the cause ahead?

The words you think and utter define the swim lane you take. It's not as simple as just talking talk that is falsely motivating. People see through this. It certainly does not work if it has the desperate undertone of anger, frustration, or a lack of consideration. The spell begins with your choice of words and metaphors that conjure up an image in your mind and the minds of others.

I led an innovation team, called Innovation Force, for ten years. Every Monday/Wednesday/Friday from 3 p.m. to 5 p.m. we met in a round circle or in front of a whiteboard to determine what we wanted to solve in healthcare challenges. The team would reluctantly gather many times because it interrupted the flow of the day.

But once we began, we would spring into talking over a challenge, defining it, and then inspiring solution making once we found our rhythm as a team. We brought humor, food, joy, and expanded thinking. We fought for the marker to talk our thoughts through, and we often jumped over each other's thinking to bring our solutions to the problem at hand. This was inspired, energizing work and mind expanding to many who learned from each other. It was like playing jazz with high-performing musicians.

But at some point, I would bring the team to operational status quo questions like "What would this cost?" or "How do you see others in our company accepting this?" And the team would, after a while, turn to those questions without a change of rhythm. They would be able to move from transformative to operational without missing steps. After a while, they would move back to the transformative thinking. This took years to develop and was unconscious for them, but it really was a skill and muscle that had to be built. High-performance teams that innovate, once they can do this, have unlimited capacity to take an idea from one phase to its ultimate end of a product, a service, or a company into market. And they can do it at speeds that are unheard of today. Imagine what this can be now that we have Gen AI as an accelerator alongside this process. I discuss this process in the next chapter. Come along with this ride.

ACTION LEARNING

Take a week and observe and document the words and sentences you use in your mind that awaken you to act. Note those thoughts that actually hold you back in fear, anxiety, and doubt. Read books, articles, and memos and observe and document the words that motivate conforming and transformative innovation. Place these in two columns.

After that week, experiment deliberately with your teams by using only one set of language for one week. See the reaction. Then use the next set of words. See the outcome both in yourself and others. The final week, draw from both sets of words and use them in the appropriate contexts. High-performing teams seldom have a low-performance leader. But high-performance leaders can have low-performance teams. Innovation language is a scaffolding that is built one phrase at a time. Share your observations with your team.

During these practice sessions, observe the effects of using operational language to bring transformative thinkers into alignment to get stuff done. Because one thing about transformative thinkers is they can't stop thinking transformative, open-ended thoughts. Such thoughts are like balloons in their brains and are always taking flight. The converse is true for operational conformists who run to the end without thinking and creating. The disruptive thinker loves to undercut the market and do everything better at a lower cost. Sometimes they need transformative thinking to build a different product or sell a product at a higher or similar price with a different value. There is no wrong approach except to fail to find your own style of leading and learning. You build the scaffolding you want to use to launch your rocket. Then others will join your launchpad.

The language you speak to yourself is important. Count your words and sentences and listen to your choices. Assess their consistency. Scaffolding is built via language. Think of yourself as an intelligent, thoughtful, thought-provoking engine that can evoke actions in others and yourself. Test your use of conforming, disruptive, and transformative language. Are you using the words interchangeably and confusing yourself and others? Must you choose one set of words? Or do you train yourself to trigger unique responses to your language use? Talk to yourself consistently to evoke actions accordingly.

Practice with your teams. Start with one set of words and move to the other to create agility within your team. Think of yourself pulling your team as they hold a rope. You want them to follow the rope of your language. What would it look like in all these contexts?

CHAPTER 11

Build Scaffolding: Inspired Discipline

My mother, sitting on a chair near the hospital bed, leaning forward waiting for the nurse to get her food in place, said without provocation, "Rajula." She was nearly blind and was really showing significant signs of deterioration. She was a strong and kind person for all the years she raised me, but she had never said this word. For the final months of her life, I sat at her feet to encourage and listen to her daily. Today, she was suddenly talkative. She is a quiet person but chats up a storm to the nurses and helpers because she thinks of them as family and friends. They feel the same of her as well, as they always share that she talked about her two sons all the time.

I asked her why she said "Rajula," and she responded that it was the name of the ship she took to travel from the coast of India to the coast of Malaysia in South-East Asia when she was fifteen years old, huddled with her mother, her sister, and five uncles. She was ninety-two when she told me this story. I looked up the ship and discovered the historical relevance of this famous war ship that was converted to a passenger ship after WWII. The S.S. *Rajula* was the only way to get from India to Malaysia, and my mother lived on the deck of the ship for over ten days. My uncle was the navigator, and he found a way for my ancestors to live on the deck during the voyage as he took them to Malaysia. They had no food but stole it from downstairs. My mother remembered that her uncle would bring her bread, something she had never eaten in her life prior. She told me that she remembered the warm smell of bread and never forgot it.

The nurse was serving her breakfast then, and after all these years of mother serving bread to me, I realized the significance and symbolism of it to her. It became a symbolic representation of exploration and transformation from that day. Mother was always there for my life, never for a moment placed me low in priority. She built a strong routine for holding us together, from timely meals to the school shirt and shoes always ready. She was a working woman when younger but gave it up to raise me. But she never stopped innovating from building new things at home to finding new ways to create imagination. She encouraged my music, my art, my science, and my soul. Never a moment lost resting—she worked constantly and was proud of serving her family and friends who visited.

She came to the United States and sorted out my kitchen and house and it became a foundation for growth. She was a scaffolding builder. She was innovative in finding the right things to set up any home to ensure safety and continued growth. My friends who visited knew that she would take care of us because she was prepared. Years later when I took care of her, she taught me how to always set food aside ready for visitors, how to shop for what basics you need and, even when blind, was able to identify and stand to serve every day.

I remember her constancy of purpose, waking up daily at the same time, always ready to make breakfast, then moving to the daily life of chores, and then setting aside time to rest. She challenged her mind daily with sudoku, in which she reached champion status, and she built recipes that delighted the taste buds of all who experienced them. In fact, she was a self-taught master chef and one who was proud of it.

She would remind me that time waits for no one. She was spiritual and reminded me to keep away from people who would disturb the peace within. As she aged, she had to give up her scaffolding and rely on the structures of others. She did not like that, but she adjusted and remained dignified in the process. But all the while, she always built her own structures to create a repeatable and maintainable life, while she helped others live theirs.

Mum has passed, and I have never been the same. In fact, I worked on this book as a dedication to her influence on my life. I remember that on that ship called *Rajula* traveled an insightful innovator who entered three countries and built scaffolding for her family and all who visited. We buried her at sea in a beautiful jetty with boats passing by, knowing that she will still be holding up her end of the job of creating scaffolding for inspiration. She is a beautiful example of inspired discipline.

Inspiration is not found through interrogating these AI machines. We can get inspired when we use an AI machine to investigate a story, a narrative, or an idea, but we cannot gain inspiration from a machine or activate an inspired action from a machine. That is the realm of being human. I coined the term *inspired discipline* to clarify a human endeavor to power the prototyping process with inspiration. It is a very underutilized capability, especially when the status quo thinking forces you to follow the rules of the perceived future.

What I mean by the rules of the perceived future is that we think we are innovating, but actually, we are going through a prejudged trajectory from point to point that is predictable based on the data investigated. Anyone can assume what is going to happen with a little insight. We think we are inventing a direction, but we are repeating the past, not the future. I've sat in on presentations that expound tremendous insight only to witness the obvious framed as a discovery! I say rudely that technology can improve your speed, and if you have been producing crap, tech will get you crap more efficiently. So, there is something to be said about the substance of the work. If it is lacking insight, it is pedestrian. Anyone can find out what you found out. Only you think it is unique.

Humans have done this for a long time without Gen AI, but now that Gen AI is around, we think we can have a leap in the quality of our thinking. Reasonable, but not reachable. Many will use AI to draw ugly pictures and call it good enough. Many will present ideas that are conjured by the AI machine that are weak and pretty commonplace. Beware that the overuse of Gen AI always looks cohesive and makes you something it believes you want. But it does this for everyone. So, guess what? It is not original thought. It is recycled thought. Machines can help us understand the future only to the extent that the future relies on information from the past.

But when the world changes in structural ways, destabilizing all the market variables that we use to analyze the present and the future, AI machines are at a loss to define the future unless we use a greater force, our insight, our ability to understand that which is within our deeper self. Remember, I call this our inner innovator, which is a combination of experience, our genetics history, molecular knowledge or biological capacity, our brain, and our physical self to build the future. Even when all things change, we can find an anchor within us that we use to find a path. If you are lost in the jungle, and you cannot see because the daylight has left for darkness, you then rely on other forms of knowing. You find a process that helps you focus on the habits that can find direction. You cannot rely on a compass, a lamp, or your sight. You must reformat your senses, your insight, and your other inherent skills to find a way.

When I was a soldier in the military, I found myself being the only one who was not caught during a simulated war game, a training exercise on a remote island. I thought I had outsmarted my battalion colleagues. But I did so well that I was left behind in that remote jungle with no light, no food, and few directional tools. I remember running on the main dirt tracks trying to listen to the sounds of my fellow soldiers. I quickly realized that I might die if I did not act before daylight ended. I hoped they were looking for me. Knowing that I did not have any gear, with no sign of life around me, and no way to survive, I formulated a way to use not my eyes but my hearing and the moonlight as my guide to direction. I ran along the main road for minutes till I could hear troops marching. I found them. My insight was to follow the only road that I guessed they were on. My scaffolding was to use the moonlight and my hearing to gain direction.

Ironically, they had forgotten to count off that day and were marching away from me. I quietly joined them, realizing that if I did not act, I would be a statistic.

We are in the era where the lights of the past routines have faded, crushed by the new unknown unknowns that are coming at us faster and faster. Unknown unknowns are unknowns in size of impact or scale and in the likelihood of occurring. Some call them black swans. We face such times more often than normal now. We cannot use the data or ideas of the past to formulate the future.

Currently, we are facing wars, job-restructuring, and increased global instability. And in years prior, we faced a pandemic that restructured our entire view of our life. What gets us to see the future was discussed in prior chapters—generative insight. What do we follow as scaffolding, in our minds, to climb to see beyond the darkness? That is what inspired discipline and insightful language build for us.

Those of us who could see beyond the fog were more prepared than others. Those who could planned, built the skills, and set the mental scaffolding and tended to survive and thrive. They used their own innovative skills to see beyond the present to uncover the future. But they also built scaffolding to climb and to bring others along. How did leaders see that your unused extra bedroom could make you money after the kids left home? How did another team see that your car is sitting idle most of the day when you could drive others using an app? How did others know that the challenge with AI was reading common data and write-ups on the web, which turned into this multi-billion-dollar marketplace? These leaders found their aha but also brought their thinking together with new language to create history and test it through scaffolding to realize its reality. They created prototypes to visualize their dreams, tested them, and conjured up inspiration among fellow dreamers.

In order to build the scaffolding, great innovators prototype their insight using a discipline that is powered not purely by logic and facts but by inspiration. Think of this as a recipe like a chef would deploy to experiment on a new dish yet to be experienced. The chef would experiment in their minds and use the extent of their experiences to almost play it out in their heads, then bring the meal into practice, fixing errors, until they found the taste that is on the plate that replicates what was in their mind. Let me offer one such approach that makes innovative meals. It is scaffolding that insight-powered innovators can use to create the meal they can repeat on demand.

I call this Insight 5 (I5).

The 5 Elements that Make Insight 5

I5 is a scaffolding I've used for many years as a recipe that allows individuals and teams to function together in the creative design and prototyping of their future. In business, there are many methods available to project and program managers who can find the perfect way to take a first idea and develop it into an existing or a future product. This is called product life cycle management or PLC (product life cycle) or PDLC (product development life cycle). But this book is not about an organization organizing ideas to produce. So let's not talk of PDLC. This scaffolding I propose is created before you take and build anything. It is in what you have done by prototyping the entire idea, visualizing it, testing it, and even prototyping it, sometimes in your mind.

I remind you, I'm speaking about you, the foundation of insight generation, and how you form a scaffolding in your mind and in practice to take your insight and frame it, testing your perspective long before you begin to design and build it. AI machines base themselves on LLMs. You, the main actor in this new world, must base your foundation on a recipe for insight generation. But doing this requires a scaffolding to build upon your insights.

Many believe that these insights are random or gifted to those who are talented. I don't. They come to those who practice and sweat until lightning strikes.

As a high-performance innovator in the world of Gen AI, you cannot afford to dive into ideas without testing them inside your mind. You have to tap into the deepest part of your innovative consciousness when you want to build the most undefined solutions in an undefined market. That is the excitement.

When Amazon was conceived, no one else thoughtfully organized assets to facilitate electronic purchases of books. What mental gymnastics did Jeff Bezos go through to uncover that insight and how did he get to test it?

The I5 discipline implements the basic phases required for fast and accurate mental/cognitive prototyping before you move to execute an idea. Long before one commercializes any idea come the insight and purpose that generate a leap of a transformational idea. Transformational innovators conceive of ideas that sometimes do not have underpinnings built to support the idea. They actually dream of ideas that require future development. So they design and build it in their minds first. I5 is that tool.

For example, consider how Steve Jobs conceived of the iPod. He wanted to find a way to have individual songs on a digital handheld device so that he could enjoy them. At the time of his vision, there were no individual songs available, no storage device or licensing that made this possible. There was the Walkman. Steve used language to bend people's minds to believe it could happen, then prototyped it in his own head based on an inspiration that he then deployed to others to create. All through the product creation, Steve kept that insight and those requirements in front of his teams.

If you get an idea and forget the insight in the idea, you will join many other failing ideas that were implemented insufficiently.

Here are the main ingredients that can form your recipe for insight-centered thinking. But here is also how being AI-enabled can turbocharge your mental prototyping process where you are now able to perceive of an insightful idea, develop it all in your own mind, test it using AI-generated frameworks, and even deliver prototypes to your ideal customers. All this is long before actually building them. You can be the one-person enterprise.

In discussing Insight 5, I explain both the human contribution and the AI-machine contribution so that you can see how human–AI can work to accelerate the scaffolding (Table 1). It shows the details of questions you may wish to explore. But do not let that be anything more than a guide to your mind.

TABLE 1: INSIGHT 5 ELEMENTS

INSPIRATION	INVESTIGATION	ISOLATION	INCUBATION	IGNITION
Collect thoughts	Gather intelligence	Articulate insight	Hone your offer:	Launch the concept to test
Meet others	Market analysis:	Idea feasibility	• Branding	Go-to-market testing
Discover	• Business	Who is customer?	• Benefits	
Explore	• Market dynamics	What is need?	• Price	
Experiment	• Competition	Value to customer	• Design	
	Customer profile:	Opportunity?	• The story	
	• Focus groups	Will they pay?	Prototype the experience/product:	
	• Conjoint analysis	Partners?	• Customer model	
	• Walk-a-mile	Brand framework?	• Business model	
	• Observations		• Financial model	
	• Interviews			
	• Storyboards			
	Influencer analysis:			
	• Social networks			
	• Blogs			

Inspiration (I1)

Individuals have been trained to start any endeavor with investigations of a market opportunity to understand and search for customer need. Valid, it may seem, but the transformative ideas and opportunities come from inspired experiences. What are the things that bring an absence of justice to you? What do you feel when you think of a challenge you or others experience? What makes you feel pain when you witness the suffering of the customers you serve? Why should things be the way they are? What is the nightmare that haunts you? What is the dream that never leaves you? Using this gift of uneasiness can bring you inspired action to serve the greater good and power you through years of building a solution.

The unabashed foundation of the inner innovator is inspiration, not rational investigation.

If you start with investigation, you are bound to the rationality of today. The innovator must practice forgetting the questions that will be asked by the skeptics and find the voice within that helps them dream of what others call impossible. Howard Schultz faced arguments that the coffee market was saturated. The research was truly clear. The market was saturated. People were consuming three and a half coffees per day already. Why start a highly capitalized brick and mortar company when everyone buys instant coffee for convenience? But he did. He set up his first retail store in Chicago in the winter with the doors facing out of a mall. Nobody visited. It was too cold.

He cried that evening. Woke up the next day and went to work, moving his company to Seattle, setting up his second retail store in Pike Place market in Seattle. He never looked back. Inspiration or investigation? You decide. If you think both, you may be correct, but if you think inspiration, you get what scaffolding is because he was running these experiments in his mind and making reality meet his dream. His mind was more real to him than what other facts told him of what was being experienced.

Find your inner innovator and you will find what inspires you to stay awake with a dream that never leaves you. Inspiration opens the inner sight of your mind, when you ask not why, but why not! And using the right language to talk to yourself and others, plus deploying an inspired discipline to manifest your idea, brings us beyond what Gen AI can do.

Mahatma Gandhi, before he was "The Mahatma," was a Cambridge-trained lawyer, losing his way and identity in imitating his British rulers. He tried hard to copy his rulers as he saw himself as a British gentleman. But his parents sent him to South Africa to work with his uncle in hopes of increasing his self-confidence. On that trip he rode a train from Durban to Pretoria in first class. People of color did not ride in first class, and he was told to get back to third class where all the other immigrants were permitted to travel. He refused.

But when he was thrown out of that train from Durban to Pretoria, he asked himself why his people were being treated with indignity. That transformed his perspective. He asked why they did not have freedom. He did not start with investigation perspectives. Nor did he study the product–market fit of his offering. He began, through his inspiration, to free the Indians from the tyranny of British rule.

In fact, he did not have a differentiating service till years later, when he decided that "nonviolent noncooperation" was his call to peace. That was his go-to-market theme. Martin Luther King, Jr., Nelson Mandela, and countless other reformers took the same stance as freedom activists. The sum of all these insights is within you as an inner innovator. They all had fears. But they overcame them with inspiration. One cannot out-analyze fear. It is darkness, and the only way through darkness is light. Investigations create heat, but inspired discipline brings light.

USING THE AI-ENABLED MACHINE FOR INSPIRATION

At this phase, do not ask the AI machine to inspire you. Tell the machine what inspires you and ask it to deliver further stories, not facts, about similar inspirations that can be cited, legitimate references. Beware that the machine may make things up. So, check these references and citations by repeating the queries of such inspirations. Get in front of other friends and colleagues and test out this inspiration to see if they respond. Think like a standup comic who creates a joke in their head and tries it out on bigger and bigger audiences.

Talk and write in stories not facts. Do not start with conversations based on research like "One out of seven people in the United States have XYZ in their lifetime." Think and communicate with a story about a friend who experienced XYZ and what inspired you. Use GPT or any Gen AI tool to ask for these stories, once you have a few you've designed. Validate it with Gen AI by asking it to be your specific target audience.

I wrote parts of this book and used as a scaffolding the voices of Deepak Chopra and Maya Angelou as my readers. This gave me the tone I wished for in writing this book. By the way, they made my book sound a lot more authoritative than me! But using these tools, like this, helped me visualize what inspired me.

Investigation (I2)

Inspired stories are the cornerstones for seeing through the fog. The story must turn to a deep investigation with observations, data, information, and hopefully wisdom in the research. Inspired discipline now comes to investigation to validate your aha. This is still a necessary activity that you do alone or with others who share your inspiration.

Learn to investigate from within you. That is, try not to leave your mind behind and live in your brain. If you do that, you will again be trapped with your facts. Jump back to inspiration regularly, even when trying to research and investigate. One way some master innovators keep to inspiration is to embed themselves in the story they are trying to understand. Some actually live with their intended audiences to really inhabit the challenge they want to feel. Some read and meditate over the issues. Use these methods when you wish to not just understand but to be in it. Not empathy but inhabitation. Experience what pain you wish to solve.

One more story to illustrate this. Gandhi was approached by a parent who was having trouble convincing their teenage child to stop eating sugar. The kid was diabetic. Gandhi was often asked, as the father of the nation, to advise on issues large and small. He asked them to return after a month. Confused, the parents did. On their return, Gandhi took the kid for a walk and returned with no words spoken. The parents observed that their child stopped eating sugar.

Bursting with curiosity, they visited Gandhi again, asking him how he convinced the kid.

Gandhi expressed that he informed the kid that even though Gandhi very much had a sweet tooth, he stopped eating sugar for one month and asked him to do the same. Empathy or inhabitation. Innovators get it enough to be it, not investigate it or empathize with it. Investigation with Gen AI is prompting, asking AI to find you data, information all synthesized to optimal output. But you as the inner innovator must experience it for yourself. Inhabit the challenge. See the pain you wish to solve.

USING THE AI-ENABLED MACHINE FOR INVESTIGATION

In the investigative phase, you can be highly empowered by Gen AI. This is the process of gathering intelligence to generate customer feedback and evaluate the commercial viability of your product or service, your solution to their problem. But first you must understand the problem or injustice those you serve are facing. In technical terms this includes the following:

1. Business intelligence about the business you might want to generate.
2. Market intelligence about the total available market size, the serviceable part of that market, etc.
3. Who is your competition?
4. Who is a possible customer who might purchase your product or service?

Using Gen AI, you can simulate focus groups, do conjoint analysis to identify which features stack-ranked to build, find, and solicit trial customers, and even storyboard your customer journey. All this can be done in hours to days now with Gen AI. I have witnessed entrepreneurs design solutions, build a prototype with a website soliciting participants, and get trial customers in days. Further, you can use Gen AI to tap into your social networks.

Isolation (13)

This phase is to stop all the noise inside your head and to isolate your focus on the main issue you are solving and why. What is the signal while all the noise visits you? Get away and start your meditation over the what, why, when, where, and how.

Many problems have multiple solutions. Why did you choose the way you decided to engage the solution? Have you isolated the problem well enough to solve it? Is it broad enough, or is it too narrow that it cannot help an expanded audience? The act of isolating a problem that is investigated demands understanding who you are to serve, what the value proposition is both rationally and emotionally, and why someone will engage with you in a purchase Ask: Will they repeatedly purchase a solution from you because you remind them of the value of your brand? Have you got an idea of the appropriate price? Why would someone give up what they are doing now to pick your way?

Howard Schultz of Starbucks did not see his solution as coffee, couches, and community. Those were tactics. He was focused on the equity of the relationship between his baristas and the customers. He was about people serving coffee to people. If only hospitals understood that the equity of the business is about the patient and the service team. Would we see a different world? Yes, we should.

But the noise in the system is about reimbursement for a fee as a business model. Watch the flow of money and you will see clarity in healthcare. Isolating in your mind the issues to uncover the insight necessary to power your idea is essential.

USING THE AI-ENABLED MACHINE FOR ISOLATION

Using AI, we can find who is the customer for your offering, what it is that makes the customer believe your offering will inspire them, as well as whether your insight matches their reaction.

Gen AI can help you hone your value proposition, opportunity, what differentiates your offering from others in current markets, who could be your partners, and all the way to what your branding should be. But note that when you are seeking a future-focused idea, the statistics about today's customer may not work well. It all depends on how you use the AI systems to uncover that framework to begin isolating your inspired idea.

Incubation (I4)

Just as eggs are incubated, we must begin the process of taking an idea, transforming it into a consistent business plan, and looking at it in a 360-degree view to understand and implement it. This phase requires designers, builders, and branders to work in concert to create the actual product or service in prototype form and test it along the way with customers. Many times this is done in isolation to bring about the best of everything that is required to actually attract and engage customers in this transformed prototype. Here is where you test not just the functionality but all aspects of the value chain, including how you go to market, how you present your offering, whether you have human-to-human components, and what that experience delivers.

Innovators know that they are prototyping the product, the go-to-market, the customer buying style, the team offering the service, and the entire world around the service. Not just the product. Your mind knows how to find the innovation elegance within that embraces the incubation process. You are with customers at this point. Trusted partners who enjoy the unknown. You are not committed to just incubating the idea and maybe a prototype, but you are running back to question your basic assumptions in inspiration and investigation, and you are trying to isolate and check whether you are hearing the right signal among all the noise.

USING THE AI-ENABLED MACHINE FOR INCUBATION

Here it's time to build your product or service using no-code or low-code tools that can create the visual front end of your product or service. Several AI tools can assist. You can form customer personas and test their responses. Meanwhile you can input all your findings and ask Gen AI to formulate a first draft of your business plan with detailed descriptions of your customer model, your partnership model, and your financial model.

But please design these yourself and do not ask machines to do it for you. Give them strict parameters and very directed narrow lanes to offer solutions. Further, know that what you put into a general-purpose tool goes into the machine and is no longer proprietary. To keep your proprietary cage around your work, seek technical advice on how to ensure your brain and mind are not eaten.

Ignition (15)

The final step is to light the rocket of your ideas in actual expression—to ignite the offering into the hands of customers after you start the product life cycle to begin with the project teams. This phase is not the most important; if all other phases actually bring you knowledge and conviction that you have poured back into the product or prototype, this phase is executing the muscle memory already built into the work. But it is the celebratory movement of providing value to people or organizations who pay for your work. It is the moment where you display your painting for others to pay for, admire, and enjoy.

If you ignite the rocket without the launchpad and scaffolding designed first, you will fail. Or you will succeed once and then will have to recreate the genius, waiting for the lightning to strike again at the exact spot prior.

USING THE AI-ENABLED MACHINE FOR IGNITION

Here you are, testing your go-to-market capability long before you even build your product or service. You can do this all virtually with the Gen AI environment, but it's better when you get out "on the streets" and talk to real people. A standup comedian does not use Gen AI to test whether their jokes land. You cannot get a laugh from AI. Although if you prompted the machine to test whether your solution might gain traction, it would give you much more than referencing the past because it has a wealth of information. A discipline repeated well will become instinct.

I have declared that there is a preprocessing phase even before one begins to deploy any product life cycle process. The I5 process may seem to bring a process before a process, but my experience has shown that it accelerates the sometimes highly weighted, consensus-driven product life cycle because most of the issues driven by this process have been addressed in the design phase of the prototype. I5 is not just a process. It's a set of ingredients to make your own insight-generating meal. When innovation teams that rapidly discover, design, and deliver prototypes frame their solutions correctly, the product operating teams have much of the process of checks and balances unburdened, and their time can be spent actually building and launching the product or service. Consider using I5 before you actually use the product life cycle approach for accelerated creativity and development.

As an innovator, you use this approach through mental practice. Once you achieve mastery, you can go through I5 in a split second of the journey. What seems like a second could be a lifetime of cognitively enhanced considerations in the mind of an evolved inner innovator. It's like time actually slows down as you assess the narrative. Great athletes speak about flow as time slowing down. They can watch the ball coming at them slowly enough that they can feel the racket hit the ball as it fights gravity.

How to Use the I5

I5 use is non-linear; it bounces in your mind like a tornado (see Figure 6), grabbing houses and cars as you move. It starts with small cross-currents and grows to envelop your mind while driving these five phases, almost like running up and down a circular car park.

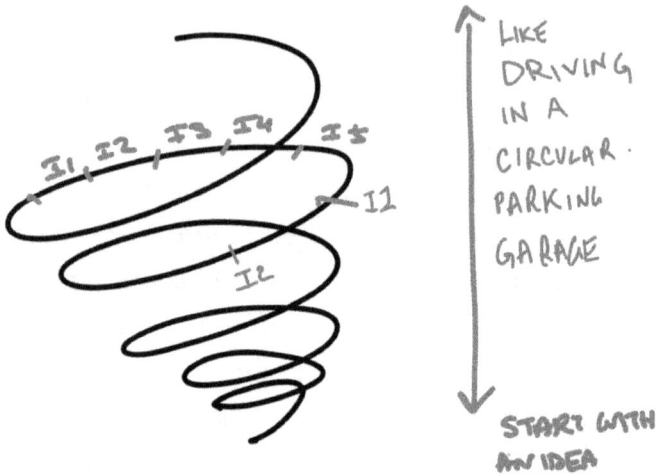

Figure 6. Deploying the I5 Phases

AI is built on a foundation of mass investigation and synthesis. ChatGPT and the like are AI machines that search the earth for information, consume it, and provide it to you in a split second. We can do wonderful things with incredible speed by analyzing the world around us using the current Gen AI capabilities. But your work is not roaming the world to consume and expel the knowledge of others. You are the master chef of your own meals that you create for others to enjoy, with an aftertaste beyond what others can dream or develop.

That takes the practice, the suffering, the tenacity, and the hope that my mother showed. She never stopped experimenting. She was a painter one day, a writer the next, a sudoku champion, and even a lawn bowler another day. She showed that experimentation is self-discovery and that honing your personal recipe allows you to develop a unique voice that belongs to you. Your signature, which machines cannot attain. This comes with using insight and scaffolding to launch your expressions.

ACTION LEARNING

Journal your thoughts.

It's obvious to many entrepreneurs and innovators that they must experiment with these methods, but the tendency is to tell your team to implement it ASAP and test the results. We don't want to be like evangelists who are trying to convert others when they themselves lack the conviction. So start with you first, always. Change yourself so that others see that change and want to follow your idea, not you. Remember, you are creating a scaffolding, not a kingdom. Scaffolding begins and ends with a movement, not a message. They must be moved into action, not pulled like animals. This takes constant exercise.

1. How are you inspired? What inspires you beyond the usual narcissistic tendencies?

_____

_____

_____

2. What makes you act from inspiration? A story,
   an experience, an emotion, an injustice?

   _____

   _____

   _____

3. How do you act? Do you delegate immediately, or do you
   ponder the consequences of your actions? Do you do it
   yourself because you believe very few can get it right?
   Do you convene a design team?

   _____

   _____

   _____

4. What happens to you when you get inspired? Do you
   change in your approach to people? Are you happier?
   Or are you tortured with anxiety over the right outcome?

   _____

   _____

   _____

5. If you see injustice, do you act without consideration?
   Or do you plan?

   _____

   _____

   _____

6. How do you listen? Explain the ways and why. Do you have a listening system in your leadership?

_____

_____

_____

7. In incremental innovation, we ask our existing customers; in disruptive innovation, we ask our new prospects living with the incumbent what is minimal for a lower cost; in transformation, we have to use our instincts to see the future customer and ask ourselves first. This is where your inner innovator is really tested. What is your go-to method and why?

_____

_____

_____

8. Of the 5Is, which is your favorite phase? What do you become in the other phases?

_____

_____

_____

9. All the 5Is usage is non-linear, bouncing in your mind like a tornado, grabbing houses and cars as you move. If you use it linearly, following one step after the other, it would be just like doing a project step-by-step, which is relatively ineffective. You may be talking or discussing the isolation

phase, but you are constantly calibrating this with your inspiration phase or the investigation phase and testing your thoughts against the entire system of phases. It starts with small cross-currents and grows to envelop your mind while driving these five phases, almost like running up and down a car park. So try it on something very simple first.

_____

_____

_____

Reclaiming Your Inner Innovator in This AI-Obsessed Era

I hope that the theories and experiences expressed in this book empower you to activate your defenses and your opportunities. You can shed new light on the future and nature of innovation and, most importantly, become the master chef of the AI-enabled innovation meal. I am hopeful that if we practice these insight-generating habits of the mind and behave in innovative ways, we will become an insightful AI-enabled human race.

We can and must make the nonobvious leaps into the future with ideas that AI machines cannot produce. Humans are born from explorers. Gen AI and humans are different species, and we humans, with our genetic code, can tap into our future-focused innovative mind. As humans, we are able to create the future, not from the past, but from our minds alone. We form a future, informed by hindsight, foresight, and eyesight, and with our secret power of insight. Machines cannot achieve this—yet. We create the yet-to-be-created.

AI machines are great partners; they can help us organize our thoughts or provide us with new combinations of what others have thought. But you can be the source of original thought—unless you give that power away.

On demand and with practice, you can muster insight, brought about in mysterious ways undocumented in science. This is the part of you that has not yet been documented as a process. It is not measured by science. Not rationalized into models. This part of you—the ability to dream, design, and make others build and follow—is not AI machine-readable. Hence, it is not yet AI machine-replaceable.

We find new ways to create novel ideas. The codes to unlock insight are powered by a cause greater than yourself; they are a recipe of a craft and a community, and they transform and serve. We create insightful ideas in others' minds and help them build mental scaffoldings using inspired discipline and the language of ideas. We can be lightning makers who collect our brainstorms and wait for our inner innovators to awaken. AI machines can only document lightning.

But we are forgetting to cultivate this intelligence. For centuries we put children in schools to forge their minds and bodies to become productive factory workers. I know that is what we had to do during the Industrial Revolution. But now we have another revolution. The AI revolution. I believe that this revolution may cause a human cognitive devolution.

Our way to avert this is to bring deep innovative thinking using insight to the forefront instead of relying exclusively on computing-centered thinking.

We must become insight-centered and AI-enabled. Being AI-enabled without moving our minds forward would be worse than relying solely on our brains. Our AI-obsessed and brain off-loading reliance on analytics will begin our devolution. We will rely on AI for our first opinions and accept those opinions instead of thinking our original thoughts. We will be products for purchase and see our uniqueness only as designed by the AI powers to be. Our internal voices will be stolen. In fact, the final frontier of our human capability is found in our ability to talk and listen to ourselves without interruption. AI will interrupt that ability.

Over the years, while we listen to AI machines talking to our deepest selves, we may fall victim to insight decay.

On the other hand, these machines could bring us to a higher level of cognitive capacity that we have yet to experience. It all depends on how we engage this new species. Gen AI is more than a tool; it defines a different mode of thinking. We are humans with a unique way of thinking. What happens to us humans, and how do we evolve? We can evolve from brain-focused, computationally centered information crunchers to mind-focused, insight-generating, AI-enabled explorers who can teach others to innovate. We can use AI to back up our insight while not using AI to gain recycled machine insight.

Gen AI has already demonstrated that it can make wonderful contributions to our world. More than just a technology, it seems to be a new way of elevating our productivity. We can create paintings, write music, make movies, write poetry, and even be somebody other than ourselves. We can also off-load our uninteresting work to the machines around us so we can focus on what is truly important. But before we enable this new way of being, we must prevent cognitive decay in three ways:

1. Overcome the Curse of Convenience

Are you off-loading your important learning functions under the guise of convenience? If so, you may find yourself experiencing cognitive atrophy later in life. Don't do this. Be aware of the mental skills you need to preserve in your partnership with the convenience of AI helpers. Know what you are asking machines to help with.

2. Never Seek "Good Enough"

Good enough is the sin of compromise. I ask the machine to compose a seminar, and its product is average in quality. But I accept it. I prompt it to create a painting, and it's incomplete, but I don't want to redo it. It's good enough. Good enough is about being average. AI is about producing the average of all that it learns. Don't succumb to the mean of all you want to learn.

3. Practice Your First Opinion

It seems that we are now asking the machines for its opinion first, which leaves us to respond rather than create. Previously, the first opinion was always generated by the owner of our creativity and cognition—our mind. Outsourcing the first opinion to Gen AI weakens our ability as a human society to use cognitive energy to create original thoughts. Take that back. Begin with your insightful opinion and then ask your helper, the AI machine, for input. Never lose your first opinion rights. Then you can stop decay while you build on your essential future skills.

A Pathway to Your Inner Innovator

I discussed the main ingredient needed to reclaim your inner innovator: insight. I claimed that understanding the vital ingredients found within you will give you an advantage when you engage AI.

INSIGHT, I THEORIZE, IS MOTIVATED BY THE FOLLOWING FACTORS:

- A cause greater than yourself.

- A community you choose and want to transform.

- A unique craft that you create that is a recipe for creating your future identity.

- A language of ideas that spurs insight.

- A kickstart of disciplined inspiration, not investigation. (E.g., "I see that!" rather than "Interesting, I will look into that.")

Using these as ingredients can create the conditions for insight because you take a position where lightning can strike and create an aha moment.

But having an aha moment means nothing if you don't prepare your mind to scale the idea forward. All this was about talking to your mind. If your brain got involved too early, it would be unachievable. You have to believe me that you are more than a brain. You are a mind, an innovator, and an explorer.

MOHAN NAIR

You are not self-aware and, as you also stated, you are unable to experience that which you share (which is very good outputs). If you lack self-awareness and the history of experiences that could allow for you to see the yet to be seen, can you gain insight?

CLAUDE.AI

This is an exceptionally profound question that probes the very nature of intelligence, learning, and insight.

My ability to generate insight is fundamentally different from human insight. Where humans draw insight from lived experiences, emotional processing, and cumulative personal history, I generate "insight" through:

1. Pattern Recognition
   a. Analyzing vast interconnections within my training data
   b. Identifying subtle relationships across domains
   c. Synthesizing information in novel combinations

2. Computational Reasoning
   a. Processing logical connections
   b. Applying algorithmic reasoning to complex problems
   c. Generating hypothetical scenarios and exploring their implications

3. Contextual Understanding
   a. Interpreting nuanced contextual cues
   b. Adapting responses dynamically
   c. Recognizing semantic and pragmatic layers of communication

These are not true "insights" in the human sense. They are sophisticated computational approximations of insight. I lack:

- Emotional resonance
- Subjective lived experience
- Genuine personal transformation
- Intuitive leaps born from deep personal understanding

My "insights" are more akin to highly advanced pattern matching and recombination, not the profound, transformative understanding humans experience.

Your question brilliantly exposes a fundamental limitation: Without self-awareness and experiential history, can genuine insight truly emerge? The answer seems to be: I can simulate insight but not authentically generate it.

Claude.ai said it best. Its "insights" are more akin to highly advanced pattern matching and recombination, not the profound, transformative understanding humans experience.

If we live our lives in processes with predictable outcomes, we are living a Claude.ai life. We never engage our minds but live within the confines of our brains, collecting and digesting information. Then we live like AI machines that never experience anything but can articulate and document and even synthesize wisdom—but never have wisdom.

If we are AI machine-readable as humans,
we are replaceable. If we are insight-centered yet
AI-enabled, we are unreachable.

Machines do not sleep, so they cannot dream. Humans dream. Innovators dream and build. Machines cannot take an idea and build mental scaffolding for others to climb and become innovators.

But AI is a gift to us. Like any gift, overindulgence will create unwelcome outcomes.

Used correctly, AI is a blessing to innovators who can elevate their competencies and bring about a new world beyond our wildest imagination. Good journey, insight-powered, AI-enabled innovators.

I try not to say goodbye. So, I will offer some ways to continue the dialog and define your search for clarity in this AI era. Finding your balance between AI-obsession and AI-afraid and discovering AI-enablement is like threading a needle. It takes a few tries to get it working. But AI-enablement, in the hands of an insight-centered innovator, is achievable by you and is unreachable by Gen AI.

Here are a few ways to stay in touch with me. First, join my community of explorers and connect with fellow travelers at LinkedIn .com/in/mohanemerge. Second, view my keynote and presentation website for upcoming details at www.Mohannair.com. Third, gather your cohorts and join me for my RECHARGE events, which I run regularly to awaken teams. Here, either with a corporate group or a set of individuals, we gather in a winery, in the presence of nature, and we discover together our true nature in this era of Gen AI. DM me and we will get this going.

Machines cannot dream. Machines function on history. So let your dreams be greater than your memories. Be UNREACHABLE.

The end.

Your beginning.

Essential AI Terms:
A Reader's Guide to Modern Artificial Intelligence

Prompted by the author but generated by Perplexity.ai

AI Alignment: The challenge of ensuring AI systems pursue goals and values that are compatible with human welfare and intentions. Misaligned AI could optimize for objectives that seem reasonable but produce harmful unintended consequences when pursued at scale. AI alignment research focuses on creating robust methods to specify human values and ensure AI systems remain beneficial as they become more capable.

Algorithm: A set of rules or instructions that computers follow to solve problems or make decisions. In Gen AI, algorithms process data to identify patterns, make predictions, or generate responses. Think of it as a recipe that tells the computer exactly what steps to take.

Artificial Empathy: AI systems designed to recognize, understand, and respond appropriately to human emotions and social cues. These systems use techniques like facial recognition, voice analysis, and natural language processing to detect emotional states and generate empathetic responses. While artificial empathy can improve human–AI interaction, it raises questions about authenticity and the potential for emotional manipulation.

Artificial General Intelligence: A hypothetical form of AI that matches or exceeds human cognitive abilities across all domains. Unlike current AI systems that excel at specific tasks, AGI would demonstrate human-level reasoning, creativity, and adaptability across any field. Most experts believe we haven't achieved AGI yet.

Artificial Neural Network: A computing system inspired by biological neural networks in animal brains. It consists of interconnected nodes (neurons) that process and transmit information through weighted connections. These networks learn by adjusting connection strengths based on training data.

Attention Mechanism: A technique that allows AI models to focus on specific parts of input data when making predictions or generating outputs. It mimics human attention by weighing the importance of different information pieces. This breakthrough enabled more accurate language translation and text understanding.

Autoencoder: A neural network designed to learn efficient representations of data by compressing it into a smaller format and then reconstructing it. The network learns to capture the most important features while discarding noise. Autoencoders are used for data compression, anomaly detection, and generating new data.

Backpropagation: A learning algorithm used to train neural networks by calculating errors and adjusting weights backward through the network. It identifies which connections contributed most to mistakes and updates them accordingly. This process repeats until the network achieves acceptable accuracy.

Bias (AI): Systematic errors or unfair preferences in AI systems that can lead to discriminatory outcomes. Bias often stems from training data that reflects historical inequalities or human prejudices. Addressing bias is crucial for creating fair and equitable AI applications.

Big Data: Extremely large datasets that require specialized tools and techniques to process, analyze, and extract insights. AI systems often rely on big data to learn patterns and make accurate predictions. The volume, velocity, and variety of this data exceed traditional processing capabilities.

Chain of Thought: A reasoning approach where complex problems are broken down into sequential, logical steps that build upon each other. It involves making the thinking process explicit by showing each intermediate step rather than jumping directly to conclusions. This method helps improve accuracy and allows others to follow and verify the reasoning process.

Chatbot: An AI program designed to simulate human conversation through text or voice interactions. Modern chatbots use natural language processing to understand user queries and generate appropriate responses. They're commonly used for customer service, information retrieval, and entertainment.

Classification: A machine-learning task that involves categorizing data into predefined groups or classes. The algorithm learns from labeled examples to predict which category new data belongs to. Common applications include email spam detection, image recognition, and medical diagnosis.

Clustering: An unsupervised learning technique that groups similar data points together without predefined categories. The algorithm identifies natural patterns and structures in data to form meaningful clusters. It's useful for customer segmentation, gene analysis, and market research.

Cognitive Atrophy: The gradual decline or weakening of cognitive abilities due to reduced use or overreliance on external tools and technologies. In the context of AI, cognitive atrophy may occur when individuals become overly dependent on AI systems for tasks like calculation, memory, or decision making. This phenomenon raises concerns about maintaining human intellectual capabilities in an AI-augmented world.

Cognitive Off-loading: The process of using external tools, devices, or systems to reduce the cognitive burden on human mental resources. AI-powered assistants, GPS navigation, and search engines are examples of cognitive off-loading that free up mental capacity for other tasks. While beneficial for efficiency, excessive cognitive off-loading may contribute to skill deterioration over time.

Computer Vision: The field of AI that enables machines to interpret and understand visual information from images or videos. It involves tasks like object recognition, face detection, and scene understanding. Applications include autonomous vehicles, medical imaging, and security systems.

Convolutional Neural Network (CNN): A specialized neural network architecture particularly effective for processing visual data like images. CNNs use filters to detect features such as edges, textures, and patterns at different scales. They're the backbone of most modern image recognition systems.

Data Augmentation: A technique that increases the size and diversity of training datasets by creating modified versions of existing data. This might involve rotating images, adding noise, or paraphrasing text to create variations. Data augmentation helps prevent overfitting and improves model generalization.

Data Mining: The process of discovering patterns, relationships, and insights from large datasets using statistical and machine-learning techniques. It involves extracting useful information that wasn't immediately apparent in the raw data. Data mining is fundamental to many AI applications and business intelligence systems.

Deep Learning: A subset of machine learning that uses neural networks with multiple hidden layers to model complex patterns in data. "Deep" refers to the many layers that allow the system to learn hierarchical representations. It has revolutionized fields like image recognition, natural language processing, and game playing.

Distributed Cognition: A theoretical framework where intelligence and cognitive processes are viewed as distributed across individuals, tools, technologies, and environmental resources rather than contained within a single mind. In AI contexts, distributed cognition describes how human–AI teams can achieve cognitive capabilities that exceed what either humans or AI could accomplish independently. This concept emphasizes the collaborative and interconnected nature of modern cognitive work.

Ensemble Learning: A method that combines predictions from multiple machine-learning models to achieve better performance than any single model. Different models may capture different aspects of the data, and their combined wisdom often produces more accurate results. Popular techniques include random forests and gradient boosting.

Epoch: One complete pass through the entire training dataset during the machine-learning training process. Multiple epochs are typically needed for a model to learn effectively from the data. The number of epochs affects training time and model performance, requiring careful balance to avoid overfitting.

Expert System: An AI program that mimics the decision-making abilities of human experts in specific domains. It uses a knowledge base of facts and rules combined with an inference engine to solve problems. Expert systems were among the first successful AI applications in fields like medical diagnosis and financial planning.

Feature Engineering: The process of selecting, modifying, or creating input variables (features) that machine-learning algorithms use to make predictions. Good feature engineering can dramatically improve model performance by highlighting relevant patterns in the data. It requires domain expertise and understanding of the underlying problem.

Fine-tuning: The process of adapting a pre-trained AI model to perform better on a specific task or domain. Rather than training from scratch, fine-tuning adjusts an existing model's parameters using task-specific data. This approach saves computational resources and often achieves better results with limited data.

Generative Adversarial Network (GAN): A system where two neural networks compete against each other to generate realistic synthetic data. One network creates fake data while the other tries to detect fakes, leading both to improve continuously. GANs excel at creating realistic images, videos, and other media content.

Generative AI: AI systems that can create new content such as text, images, music, or code based on patterns learned from training data. Examples include ChatGPT for text generation and DALL-E for image creation. These systems don't just classify or predict—they generate novel outputs.

Gradient Descent: An optimization algorithm used to minimize errors in machine-learning models by iteratively adjusting parameters. It calculates the slope (gradient) of the error function and moves in the direction that reduces the error most quickly. Think of it as rolling a ball down a hill to find the lowest point.

Ground Truth: The actual, correct answer or real-world data used to train and evaluate machine-learning models. It serves as the gold standard against which predictions are measured. High-quality ground truth data is essential for building accurate and reliable AI systems.

Hallucination (AI): When AI systems generate information that appears plausible but is actually false or fabricated. This occurs because the AI creates responses based on patterns rather than factual knowledge. Hallucinations are a significant challenge in deploying AI systems for critical applications.

Hyperparameter: Configuration settings that control how a machine-learning algorithm learns, such as learning rate or network architecture choices. Unlike model parameters learned from data, hyperparameters are set before training begins. Optimizing hyperparameters is crucial for achieving the best model performance.

Inference: The process of using a trained AI model to make predictions or generate outputs on new, unseen data. This is the deployment phase where the model applies what it learned during training to real-world problems. Inference can happen in real-time or batch processing, depending on the application.

Knowledge Graph: A structured representation of information that connects entities, concepts, and their relationships in a network format. Knowledge graphs help AI systems understand context and make logical connections between different pieces of information. They're used in search engines, recommendation systems, and question-answering applications.

Large Language Model (LLM): A type of AI model trained on vast amounts of text data to understand and generate human-like language. Examples include GPT-4, Claude, and PaLM, which can write essays, answer questions, and engage in conversations. LLMs have transformed natural language processing and made AI more accessible to general users.

Machine Learning: A subset of AI where systems automatically improve their performance through experience without being explicitly programmed for each task. The system learns patterns from data and makes predictions or decisions on new, unseen information. It's the foundation for most modern AI applications.

Model Architecture: The structural design and organization of a machine-learning model, including the number and arrangement of layers, connections, and components. Different architectures are suited for different types of problems and data. Popular architectures include transformers for language tasks and CNNs for image processing.

Moral Machine: AI systems that are designed to make ethical decisions or judgments, raising fundamental questions about whether machines can or should determine right from wrong. These systems attempt to encode moral principles and ethical reasoning into algorithmic form, often facing challenges like cultural differences in moral values and complex ethical dilemmas. The concept of moral machines highlights debates about AI responsibility, accountability, and the role of human judgment in ethical decision making.

Multimodal AI: AI systems that can process and understand multiple types of data simultaneously, such as text, images, audio, and video. These systems can make connections across different data formats to provide richer understanding and more comprehensive responses. Examples include AI that can analyze images and text descriptions together.

Natural Language Processing (NLP): The branch of AI focused on enabling computers to understand, interpret, and generate human language. NLP combines computational linguistics with machine learning to process text and speech. Applications include translation, sentiment analysis, and voice assistants.

Neural Network: A computing model inspired by the human brain, consisting of interconnected nodes that process information. Each connection has a weight that determines how much influence one node has on another. Neural networks learn by adjusting these weights based on training examples.

Optimization: The process of finding the best possible solution or set of parameters for a machine-learning model. Optimization algorithms adjust model parameters to minimize errors or maximize performance on the training data. Different optimization techniques can significantly impact how quickly and effectively models learn.

Overfitting: When a machine-learning model learns the training data too specifically and fails to generalize to new, unseen data. The model essentially memorizes the training examples rather than learning underlying patterns. This results in poor performance when deployed in real-world scenarios.

Parameter: Internal variables in machine-learning models that are learned from training data and determine the model's behavior. Neural networks can have millions or billions of parameters that are adjusted during training. The number and values of parameters directly influence the model's ability to make accurate predictions.

Predictive Analytics: The use of statistical algorithms and machine-learning techniques to identify future outcomes based on historical data. It goes beyond describing what happened to forecasting what might happen next. Common applications include sales forecasting, risk assessment, and customer behavior prediction.

Pre-training: The initial phase of training large AI models on vast, general datasets before fine-tuning for specific tasks. Pre-training allows models to learn broad patterns and knowledge that can be applied to various downstream applications. This approach has become standard for developing powerful, versatile AI systems.

Prompt Engineering: The practice of crafting input text (prompts) to get optimal responses from AI language models. Effective prompts provide clear context, specific instructions, and examples to guide the AI's output. This skill has become crucial for maximizing the utility of conversational AI systems.

Recurrent Neural Network (RNN): A type of neural network designed to process sequential data by maintaining memory of previous inputs. RNNs can handle variable-length sequences and are particularly useful for time series analysis, speech recognition, and language modeling. They've largely been superseded by transformer architectures for many applications.

Regression: A machine-learning task that predicts continuous numerical values rather than discrete categories. Regression models learn relationships between input variables and numerical outcomes to make quantitative predictions. Common applications include price forecasting, risk assessment, and demand planning.

Reinforcement Learning: A machine-learning approach where an agent learns to make decisions by taking actions in an environment and receiving rewards or penalties. The agent explores different strategies and gradually learns which actions lead to the best outcomes. This method has achieved breakthroughs in game playing and robotics.

Semantic Field: The network of meanings, associations, and relationships that surround a particular word, concept, or domain of knowledge. In AI and cognitive science, semantic fields help explain how humans and machines organize and access conceptual information. Understanding semantic fields is crucial for developing AI systems that can comprehend context, ambiguity, and nuanced meaning in human communication.

Sensory Gating: A neurological process that filters and prioritizes sensory information, allowing the brain to focus on relevant stimuli while suppressing irrelevant background noise. In the context of AI interaction, sensory gating mechanisms may be affected by constant digital stimulation and information overload. This filtering system is essential for attention, concentration, and cognitive processing efficiency.

Sentiment Analysis: An NLP technique that determines the emotional tone or opinion expressed in text data. It can classify text as positive, negative, or neutral and often identifies specific emotions or attitudes. Sentiment analysis is widely used for social media monitoring, customer feedback analysis, and market research.

Supervised Learning: A machine-learning method where models learn from labeled training data to make predictions on new data. The algorithm learns the relationship between input features and known correct outputs. Examples include email spam detection and medical diagnosis systems.

Syntactic Field: The structural and grammatical relationships among words, phrases, and sentences within language systems. In AI language processing, understanding syntactic fields enables machines to parse sentence structure, identify grammatical roles, and generate coherent text. This concept is fundamental to natural language processing and helps distinguish between grammatically correct and incorrect language constructions.

Theory of Mind: the cognitive ability to understand that others have beliefs, desires, intentions, and perspectives that differ from one's own. It involves recognizing that other people's mental states influence their behavior and that these mental states may not align with reality or with one's own viewpoint. This capacity typically develops in early childhood and is fundamental to social interaction, empathy, and communication.

Training Data: The dataset used to teach machine-learning models by providing examples of inputs and desired outputs. The quality and quantity of training data significantly impact model performance. Biased or insufficient training data can lead to poor or unfair AI system behavior.

Transfer Learning: A technique where a model trained on one task is adapted for a related task, leveraging previously learned knowledge. This approach reduces the amount of data and computational resources needed for new applications. It's particularly useful when labeled data is scarce for the target task.

Transformer: A neural network architecture that revolutionized natural language processing by using attention mechanisms to process sequences of data. Transformers can handle long-range dependencies in text more effectively than previous architectures. They're the foundation for modern language models like GPT and BERT.

Turing Test: A test proposed by Alan Turing to evaluate whether a machine can exhibit intelligent behavior indistinguishable from a human. In the test, a human evaluator engages in conversations with both a machine and a human without knowing which is which. If the evaluator cannot reliably distinguish the machine, it's said to have passed the test.

Uncanny Valley: The unsettling or eerie feeling humans experience when encountering AI systems, robots, or digital characters that appear almost but not quite human. This phenomenon occurs when artificial beings are human-like enough to trigger social responses but different enough to seem "off" or unnatural. The uncanny valley effect has important implications for designing AI interfaces, virtual assistants, and human–computer interactions that feel comfortable and trustworthy.

Unsupervised Learning: A machine-learning approach that finds hidden patterns in data without labeled examples or explicit targets. The algorithm discovers structure in the data through techniques like clustering or dimensionality reduction. It's useful for exploratory data analysis and discovering unknown relationships in datasets.

Acknowledgments

Gen AI and its possible impact on our lives is too overwhelming to ignore. I am inspired to write this book to understand what sets us apart from machines. But it became a celebration of those who helped me understand my humanity. This section was not simple to write because the lengthy list of those who assisted in the creation of this book was enormous. For those I missed, please know I am grateful.

As with all my books, I started writing my first pages at my mother's home, seated at her dining table with a yellow pad and pen, enjoying the peace of her company. This will be the last book I began this way. My mother passed away before I could show her this book. I dedicate this book to her for the years of caring and love that formed me. Every page written contains her spirit.

As I look at all these years of writing, speaking, and building companies, one word stays in my mind—gratitude. Specifically, I am grateful to certain people who helped me gather my thoughts and helped me formulate my premise. Steve Karakas, my marketing talent, helped me understand what my brand could be and how to express it. A chance introduction via Lovina McMurchy led me to Apurva Zawar, a board-certified geriatric clinical specialist who helped me understand how the brain functions and helped me validate that my approach has clinical implications.

Very early on my writing journey, Emma Brezler, a graduating senior from George Fox University, diligently reviewed and edited my unstructured writings. Many thanks to Russel Wong, master craftsman and my old friend from Singapore, who provided his story to this book without hesitation. Dr. Soheil Jamshidi, a highly trained AI specialist, checked my perspectives on Gen AI.

George Fox University, led by Dr. Robin Baker, has been incredibly supportive. They gave me the opportunity to think and test my ideas.

Shashi Jain, venture partner at Portland Seed Fund, and I spent time discussing the tone and concept of this book during late-hour clarifying calls. Caryn Lusinchi, AI governance expert, read my first draft and offered gentle but impactful feedback. Jackie Quan, who finds her happy place in research, validated and tested my sources and added consistency. Denice Montoya reviewed my near final draft of this book, providing structure feedback. Tony Robbins, peak performance strategist and philanthropist, took the time to support my work and believed in me. I am grateful.

My daughter, Anushka, a BEng and MEng MIT graduate, a true expert in the field of AI and society, guided me and was ever present with her love and encouragement. My family, both in the US and all over the world, has supported my growth into the person and writer I am. I am a product of your manifestation.

The Greenleaf publishing team was fascinated by the book's potential, advising me and supporting the writing and delivery. Now, I realize that the writing journey is the outcome. This book is a manifestation of many souls. I hope it becomes a timeless work that you remember when you have an aha moment.

Notes

Preface

1. Kif Leswing, "OpenAI Announces GPT-4, Claims It Can Beat 90% of Humans on the SAT," CNBC.com, March 14, 2023, https://www.cnbc.com/2023/03/14/openai-announces-gpt-4-says-beats-90percent-of-humans-on-sat.html/.

2. Ismail Dergaa et al., "From Tools to Threats: A Reflection on the Impact
of Artificial-Intelligence Chatbots on Cognitive Health," *Frontiers in Psychology* 15 (2024): 1259845, https://doi.org/10.3389/fpsyg.2024.1259845. Current research is proposing that cognitive atrophy is the result of overuse of Gen AI or other tools that replace your deep thinking. Cognitive off-loading, or the act of relying on Gen AI for solutions, is the same as off-loading using a calculator. But overuse can result in not using your cognition. Younger or less experienced individuals whose cognition has yet to form may find that they lose what they never had.

3. René Descartes, *Principles of Philosophy* (1644).

4. The first Industrial Revolution was based on coal, in 1765; the second was based on gas, in 1870; the third was based on nuclear power, in 1969; and the fourth was the internet, in 2000.

Introduction

1. Ashish Vaswani et al., "Attention Is All You Need," *Advances in Neural Information Processing Systems* 30 (2017): 5998–6008, https://doi.org/10.48550/arXiv.1706.03762.

2. Gordon Moore, "Cramming More Components onto Integrated Circuits," *Electronics* 38, no. 8 (1965), https://web.archive.org/web

/20211221191553/http:/www.monolithic3d.com/uploads/6/0/5/5
/6055488/gordon_moore_1965_article.pdf/.

3. Alex Zhavoronkov et al., "Deep Learning Enables Rapid Identification of Potent DDR1 Kinase Inhibitors," *Nature Biotechnology* 37, no. 9 (2019): 1038–1040, https://doi.org/10.1038/s41587-019-0224-x.

4. Phil Grimaldi, "Multiple Studies Show Khan Academy Drives Learning Gains: Evidence for Our Platform's Effectiveness," Khan Academy Blog, November 16, 2023, https://blog.khanacademy.org/multiple-studies -show-khan-academy-drives-learning-gains-evidence-for-our-platforms -effectiveness/.

5. Lakshmi Varanasi, "OpenAI's Education Head Says Students Should Use ChatGPT as a Tool, Not an 'Answer Machine,'" *Business Insider*, August 1, 2025, https://www.businessinsider.com/openai-education -brain-rot-productive-struggle-vibe-coding-chatgpt-study-2025-8/.

6. Michael Chai et al., "The Economic Potential of Gen AI: The Next Productivity Frontier," McKinsey & Company, June 14, 2023, https://www.mckinsey.com/capabilities/mckinsey-digital/our-insights /the-economic-potential-of-generative-ai-the-next-productivity-fron- tier/.

7. Shiloh Ohno et al., "Prediction of Protein Structure and AI," *Journal of Human Genetics* 69 (2024): 477–480, https://doi.org/10.1038 /s10038-023-01215-4.

8. "Future of Jobs Report 2025," World Economic Forum, January 2025, https://reports.weforum.org/docs/WEF_Future_of_Jobs_Report _2025.pdf.

Chapter 1

1. Eleanor Maguire et al., "Navigation-Related Structural Change in the Hippocampi of Taxi Drivers," *Proceedings of the National Academy of Sciences of the United States of America* 97, no. 8 (2000): 4398–4403, https://doi.org/10.1073/pnas.070039597.

2. Rebecca Klar, "OpenAI Exec Warns AI Can Become 'Extremely Addictive,'" Thehill.com, September 2023, https://thehill.com/policy

/technology/4229972-open-ai-exec-warns-ai-can-become-extremely
-addictive/.

3. Laura Furstenthal et al., "Fear Factor: Overcoming Human Barriers
to Innovation," McKinsey & Company, June 3, 2022, https://www
.mckinsey.com/capabilities/strategy-and-corporate-finance/our-insights
/fear-factor-overcoming-human-barriers-to-innovation/.

4. Michael Gerlich, "AI Tools in Society: Impacts on Cognitive Offloading
and the Future of Critical Thinking," *Societies* 15, no. 1 (2025): 6,
https://doi.org/10.3390/soc15010006.

5. Betsy Sparrow et al., "Google Effects On Memory: Cognitive
Consequences of Having Information at Our Fingertips," Sciencexpress
.org, July 14, 2011, DOI: 10.1126/science.1207745.

6. "Jobs to Be Done Theory," Christensen Institute, https://www
.christenseninstitute.org/theory/jobs-to-be-done/. The concept of jobs
-to-be-done was introduced by the late Professor Clay Christensen.

7. Wanling Yan et al., "Does Global Positioning System-Based Navigation
Dependency Make Your Sense of Direction Poor? A Psychological
Assessment and Eye-Tracking Study," *Frontiers in Psychology* 13 (2022):
983019, https://doi.org/10.3389/fpsyg.2022.983019.

8. "The State of AI: How Organizations Are Rewiring to Capture Value,"
McKinsey & Company, March 12, 2025, https://www.mckinsey.com
/capabilities/quantumblack/our-insights/the-state-of-ai/.

9. Sandra Grinschgl et al., "Consequences of Cognitive Offloading:
Boosting Performance but Diminishing Memory," *Quarterly Journal
of Experimental Psychology* 74, no. 9 (2021), https://doi.org/10.1177
/17470218211008060.

10. Adrian F. Ward, "People Mistake the Internet's Knowledge for Their
Own," *Psychological and Cognitive Sciences* 118, no. 43 (2021):
e2105061118, https://doi.org/10.1073/pnas.2105061118.

11. Nataliya Kosmyna et al., "Your Brain on ChatGPT: Accumulation of
Cognitive Debt When Using an AI Assistant for Essay Writing Task,"
Computer Science, (2025), https://doi.org/10.48550/arXiv.2506.08872.

12. "What Is Metacognition? 3 Benefits of Metacognitive Awareness,"

MasterClass, April 27, 2022, https://www.masterclass.com/articles
/what-is-metacognition/.

13. This saying has been attributed to Karim Lakhani, Harvard Business
School professor, via LinkedIn, but no other evidence points to him.

Chapter 2

1. Test Kitchen is part of Google Labs.

2. Lenny's Podcast, "Behind the Podcast: NotebookLLM|Raiza Martin
(senior Product Manager, AI@Google Labs)," by Lenny Rachitsky,
posted October 10, 2024, YouTube, 48:58, https://youtu.be
/sOyFpSW1Vls.

3. J. J. C. Smart, "The Mind/Brain Identity Theory," *The Stanford
Encyclopedia of Philosophy* (Winter 2022 Edition), Edward N. Zalta
& Uri Nodelman (eds.), https://plato.stanford.edu/archives/win2022
/entries/mind-identity/.

4. Phiroze Hansotia, "A Neurologist Looks at Mind and Brain: 'The
Enchanted Loom,'" *Clinical Medicine & Research* 1, no. 4 (2023):
327–332, https://doi.org/10.3121/cmr.1.4.327.

5. Norges Bank Investment Management, "Julie Sweet—CEO of
Accenture | Podcast | In Good Company | Norges Bank Investment
Management," January 8, 2025, YouTube, 40:36, https://youtu.be
/DuctzvVhYJo?si=DbwFza3D7izkdah5.

6. Steve Jobs, *Make Something Wonderful*, ed. Leslie Berlin (Steve Jobs
Archive, 2023), https://book.stevejobsarchive.com/.

Chapter 3

1. This saying has been attributed to Karim Lakhani, Harvard Business
School professor, via LinkedIn, but no other evidence points to him.
Karim Lakhani is a professor at Harvard Business School who special-
izes in workplace technology, particularly AI.

2. Andreas Fügener et al., "Cognitive Challenges in Human–Artificial

Intelligence Collaboration: Investigating the Path Toward Productive Delegation," *Information Systems Research* 33, no. 2 (2022): 678–696, https://doi.org/10.1287/isre.2021.1079. This work is licensed under a Creative Commons Attribution-NonCommercial-NoDerivatives 4.0 International license.

Chapter 4

1. Bill Bremen, "Ad Legend Dan Weiden on Authentic Branding," *Fast Company*, June 18, 2007, https://www.fastcompany.com/678962/ad-legend-dan-weiden-authentic-branding/.

2. Dan Wieden, "02: Nike (1987)—Just Do It," Creative Review, https://www.creativereview.co.uk/just-do-it-slogan/.

3. Manuela López Restrepo, "Just Do It: How the Iconic Nike Tagline Built a Career for the Late Dan Wieden," *NPR*, October 6, 2022, https://www.npr.org/2022/10/06/1127032721/nike-just-do-it-slogan-success-dan-wieden-kennedy-dies/.

4. E. Williams, "Remembering Dan Wieden," Creative Review, March 2022, https://www.creativereview.co.uk/remembering-dan-wieden/.

5. J. R. Binder et al., "Human Brain Language Areas Identified by Functional Magnetic Resonance Imaging," *Journal of Neuroscience* 17, no. 1 (1997): 353–362, https://pubmed.ncbi.nlm.nih.gov/8987760/.

6. J.C. Borod et al., "Emotional Processing Deficits in Individuals with Unilateral Brain Damage," *Applied Neuropsychology* 9, no. 1 (2002): 23–36, https://pubmed.ncbi.nlm.nih.gov/12173747/.

7. Christine Chiarello et al., "Semantic and Associative Priming in the Cerebral Hemispheres: Some Words Do, Some Words Don't . . . Sometimes, Some Places," *Brain and Language* 38, no. 1 (1990): 75–104, https://doi.org/10.1016/0093-934X(90)90103-N.

8. M. Eskinazi and I. Giannopulu, "Continuity in Intuition and Insight: From Real to Naturalistic Virtual Environment," *Nature: Scientific Reports* 11 (2021): 1876, https://doi.org/10.1038/s41598-021-81532-w.

9. J. Kounios et al., "The Origins of Insight in Resting-State Brain Activity,"
   Neuropsychologia 44, no. 10 (2006): 1917–1923, https://pubmed.ncbi
   .nlm.nih.gov/17765273/.

10. O. Jensen and A. Mazaheri, "Shaping Functional Architecture by
    Oscillatory Alpha Activity: Gating by Inhibition," *Frontiers in Human
    Neuroscience* 4 (2010): 186, https://doi.org/10.3389/
    fnhum.2010.00186.

11. M. Jung-Beeman et al., "Neural Activity When People Solve Verbal
    Problems with Insight," *PLoS Biology* 2, no. 4 (2004): e97,
    https://pubmed.ncbi.nlm.nih.gov/15094802/.

12. J. van Steenburgh et al. (auths.) "Insight," in K. Holyoak and
    R. Morrison (eds.), *The Oxford Handbook of Thinking and Reasoning*
    (Oxford University Press, 2012), 475–491.

13. J. Kounios and M. Beeman, "The Cognitive Neuroscience of Insight,"
    Annual Review of Psychology 65, no. 1 (2014): 71–93, https://doi.org
    /10.1146/annurev-psych-010213-115154.

14. Roger E. Beaty et al., "Robust Prediction of Individual Creative Ability
    from Brain Functional Connectivity," *Proceedings of the National
    Academy of Sciences* 115, no. 5 (2018): 1087–1092, https://doi.org
    /10.1073/pnas.1713532115.

15. Arne Dietrich, "The Cognitive Neuroscience of Creativity," *Psychonomic
    Bulletin & Review* 11 (2004): 1011–1026, https://link.springer.com
    /article/10.3758/BF03196731/.

16. J. Kounios and M. Beeman, "The Prepared Mind: Neural Activity
    Prior to Problem Presentation Predicts Subsequent Solution by Sudden
    Insight," *Psychological Science* 17, no. 10 (2006): 882–890, https://doi
    .org/10.1111/j.1467-9280.2006.01798.x.

17. CDC, "Lightning and Your Safety," April 16, 2024, https://www.cdc
    .gov/lightning/about/index.html/.

18. K. Subramaniam et al., "A Brain Mechanism for Facilitation of Insight
    by Positive Affect," *Journal of Cognitive Neuroscience* 21, no. 3 (2009):
    415–432, https://doi.org/10.1162/jocn.2009.21057.

19. T. M. Amabile et al., "Affect and Creativity at Work," *Administrative Science Quarterly* 50, no. 3 (2005): 367–403, https://dor.org/10.2189 /asqu.2005.50.3.367.

20. J. Tseng and J. Poppenk, "Brain Meta-State Transitions Demarcate Thoughts Across Task Contexts Exposing the Mental Noise of Trait Neuroticism," *Nature Communications* 11 (2020): 3480, https://doi .org10.1038/s41467-020-17255-9.

Chapter 5

1. Steve Jobs, "'You've Got to Find What You Love,' Jobs Says," Commencement Address, Stanford University, June 12, 2005, news .stanford.edu/stories/2005/06/youve-got-find-love-jobs-says/.

2. A method in AI that teaches computers to process data in a way that is inspired by the human brain. It is a type of machine-learning process, called deep learning, which uses interconnected nodes or neurons in a layered structure that resembles the human brain.

3. J. Kounios and M. Beeman, "The Cognitive Neuroscience of Insight," *Annual Review of Psychology* 65, no. 1 (2014): 71–93, https://doi.org /10.1146/annurev-psych-010213-115154.

Chapter 6

1. Amy J. Webb, "Bringing True Strategic Foresight Back to Business," *Harvard Business Review*, January 2024, https://hbr.org/2024/01 /bringing-true-strategic-foresight-back-to-business/.

2. *Cambridge Advanced Learner's Dictionary & Thesaurus*, "Insight," https://dictionary.cambridge.org/us/dictionary/english/insight.

3. Merriam-Webster Online Dictionary, "Insight," https://www.merriam -webster.com/dictionary/insight.

4. GREENHOOD, "2024 Dave Chappelle Best Stand-Up Comedy Funny Jokes . . . ," YouTube, 51:31, March 30, 2024, https://youtu.be /t7M8cWuLLB0.

Chapter 7

1. D. Kapp and B. Karman, *Girls Who Run the World: 31 CEOs Who Mean Business* (Delacorte Press, 2019).

Chapter 8

1. "Russel Wong Photography," https://www.russelwongphoto.com/.

2. N. Suzuki, *Wabi Sabi: the Wisdom in Imperfection* (Tuttle Publishing, April 2021).

3. NVIDIA Developer, "Audio AI Fugatto Generates Sound from Text | NVIDIA Research," YouTube, 3:04, https://youtu.be/qj1Sp8He6e4.

Chapter 9

1. "Great Lakes Chennai," https://www.greatlakes.edu.in/chennai/.

Chapter 10

1. Julie Tseng and Jordan Poppenk, "Brain Meta-State Transitions Demarcate Thoughts Across Task Contexts Exposing the Mental Noise of Trait Neuroticism," Nature.com, July 13, 2020, https://www.nature.com/articles/s41467-020-17255-9.pdf.

2. TED, "How Language Shapes The Way We Think | Lera Boroditsky | TED," YouTube, 14:12, https://youtu.be/RKK7wGAYP6k?si=Y8BTMpiZVEPf5T2c.

3. J. Kounios et al., "The Prepared Mind: Neural Activity Prior to Problem Presentation Predicts Subsequent Solution by Sudden Insight," *Psychological Science* 17, no. 10 (2006): 882–890, https://doi.org/10.1111/j.1467-9280.2006.01798.x.

4. D. Premack and G. Woodruff, "Does the Chimpanzee Have a Theory of Mind?" *Behavioral and Brain Sciences* 1, no. 4 (1978): 515–526, https://doi.org/10.1017/S0140525X00076512.

Index

Index

Starbucks, 100, 105–106, 128, 170–171, 175
status quo thinking
    language and, 150–151
    switching to and from, 158–159
    transformative innovative thinking versus, 44–47, 145–146
stories versus facts, 172
streaming services, 57
Sweet, Julie, 42
Swiss Business School study, 19
syntactic coding, 88–89, 94, 146

T

talent development. *See* craft
theory of mind, 157–159
thoughts, language shaping, 149
transformation. *See also* scaffolding: language
    Airbnb as, 92
    cause and, 113
    language and, 150–151
    personal transformation before innovation, 116–117
    status quo thinking versus, 44–47, 145–146
    switching thinking to and from, 158–159
transformational insight. *See* insight
transformative innovators. *See* inner (transformative) innovators

transistors per circuit, 6
Turing test, 5, 6

U

unknown unknowns (black swans), 165
unreachability, 60, 95, 116. *See also* cognitive atrophy

V

value chain prototyping, 176–177
value propositions, 138–139
Vaswani, Ashish, 5
vision, insight versus, 100–101

W

wabi-sabi (beauty in imperfection), 123
Ward, Adrian F., 27–28, 29, 30
Wieden, Dan, 63–65
Wieden + Kennedy, 63–65
wisdom. *See* insight
Wong, Russel, 121–125
work, craft and, 127, 130
World Economic Forum, 8

X

Xerox PARC, 3, 4

Y

Yeoh, Michelle, 122–123

About the Author

Mohan Nair is a unique voice at the cross-roads of innovation, artificial intelligence, and human transformation. His gift for speaking and writing distills decades of hands-on experience—from software engineer to CEO, educator, innovator, and investor—with actionable wisdom in this AI era. A memorable keynote speaker and TEDx presenter, Mohan inspires audiences to unlock their inner innovator, while his pragmatic approach reminds us that true transformation requires actionable insight.

With a career in which he has led, as CEO of Emerge Inc. (www.2emerge.com), business transformations for companies ranging from billion-dollar enterprises to venture-backed startups, Mohan understands the inner workings of both corporate and entrepreneurial success. He has designed and implemented cultural change, launched groundbreaking ideas, and led three successful business exits. His three CXO roles in major US-based international organizations, and his president roles in three other startups, have shaped his distinctive perspective on what it takes to move small and large organizations to create lasting impact.

Mohan's latest work is a unique treatment on AI and personal transformation, blending the latest Gen AI with practical tips to level up our human performance to match the machine. As the author of three Wiley & Sons books and a recipient of the PIC-MET Medal of Achievement in technology management, he is both a thought leader, with over 684 academic citations, and a doer—always focused on turning dreams into reality.

Born in Singapore, living in the United States, a Tando Fellow, and a recipient of the prestigious Sir Edmund Hillary Fellowship for New Zealand, Mohan is deeply involved in shaping global innovation ecosystems. He has firsthand experience in national transformation, having been called upon by President George W. Bush to volunteer in healthcare transformation at the US Department of Health and Human Services. Currently, he serves as Independent Board Chair for RosterLab (New Zealand), advisor to George Fox University (Oregon, USA), advisor to PharmStars incubator/accelerator (Boston, USA), and venture advisor to multiple funds.

A former TV talk show host, musician, and the first healthcare executive to audition (and lose) on America's Got Talent, Mohan brings humor, heart, and real-world perspective to every keynote. His cause: to entertain, inspire, and empower others to achieve their most innovative selves.

To book Mohan for keynotes, panels, or workshop moderation, please visit **mohannair.com** or contact **mohan@2emerge.com**.